Negotiating With Agility

Negotiating With Agility

A Manager's Guide to Better Labor Agreements

Kathy Beyerchen

Leader in applied, concise business books

First published in 2023 by
Business Expert Press, LLC
222 East 46th Street, New York, NY 10017
www.businessexpertpress.com

ISBN-13: 978-1-63742-471-1 (paperback)
ISBN-13: 978-1-63742-472-8 (e-book)

Business Expert Press Human Resource Management and Organizational Behavior Collection

First edition: 2023

10 9 8 7 6 5 4 3 2 1

*To my negotiations mentors. First, Jim Gomes who demonstrated
to me the critical role personal integrity plays in labor agreement
negotiations. When he entered the room, every negotiator on both sides
of the table literally stood up with respect. Second, Bert Birdsall, Jr. whose
personal integrity and joy of storytelling are with me today. And third,
Len Hecht, a negotiator's negotiator; master of stillness, details, and agility.*

Description

At last, a concise, practical guide that shows managers how to create agility at the bargaining table through thoughtful planning and preparation in the weeks, months, *and years before* formal negotiations begin, and how to do that on top of your regular full-time job. This is the work that you don't have the luxury of doing *during* negotiations. It is either done in advance or it is not done. It is the foundation on which agility is built. Absent this effort, your organization will be saddled with unnecessary costs and inefficient work processes. And with the strength of an informed contract, management's relationship with its union should improve and the resulting collective bargaining agreement (CBA) can be expected to be well received by the union, its members, your supervisors, and your managers.

Agility in labor agreement negotiations is the ability to recognize and respond in the moment to threats and opportunities, both anticipated and unexpected. Agility gives you the confidence to talk with a party you may or may not be able to trust, and have a conversation the outcome of which will significantly impact your company and future CBAs. Agility allows you to pivot.

Keywords

labor negotiations; CBA negotiations; labor contract; labor agreement; labor relations; industrial relations

Contents

Testimonials

"There is nothing else out there like this ... I loved the tools and content included in this important work and recommend it to anyone. While it is especially helpful to those newer to contract negotiations, it also provides excellent structure and ideas that even seasoned negotiators will appreciate!" **—Melinda Rogers, Chief Human Resources and Diversity Officer, NW Natural**

"I especially like the way the author organizes the process, provides real life examples, and reports outcomes. This book is neither too colloquial nor too technical, and will be immediately useful to seasoned negotiators and newbies alike." **—Cyndi Sauter, President and CEO, Burdzinski & Partners, Inc. (labor relations specialists)**

Acknowledgments

Writing for a commercial publication is a different animal compared to the in-house writing I have always done or the regular marketing letters I wrote years ago when I had my own business. Special thanks to Cyndi Sauter who first suggested the idea of reporting my approach. I'm grateful to Melinda Rogers and Dawn Blessing who gave their enthusiastic support throughout the process. And, of course, my never-ending appreciation to my husband, Alan Beyerchen, who always believed I could tame this beast. Over the years, I have witnessed Alan write professionally and coach others in their writings. What a delight it has been to have him sitting across from me encouraging me to find my voice and tell just one more story. *Akai ito* is ours.

Introduction

Agility in labor agreement negotiations is the ability to recognize and respond in real time to threats and opportunities, both anticipated and unexpected. Agility means you are confident in your ability to talk with a party you may or may not be able to trust, and to have a conversation the outcome of which will impact your company and future collective bargaining agreements for years into the future. The outcome of your bargaining conversation will expand or contract your ability to manage future costs and operational processes.

This guide is about the planning and preparation work that management needs to do in the weeks and months and *years before bargaining* begins, and which needs to be done in order to create the agility that is needed to effectively negotiate a collective bargaining agreement (CBA). A superior negotiator will prepare deeply throughout the entire life cycle of the labor contract in order to make the next round of bargaining more efficient and more effective. And yet, most do not invest the time needed to be truly effective. Why? Because they can't see how to do all that work on top of their already full-time jobs. This guide walks you through how to map out all the work that needs to happen on top of your regular work.

Each proposed preparation step is described including when it should happen, why, and how. You select the steps you wish to use based on your organization's needs and the context in which you will be bargaining.

Absent this work, your organization will be saddled with unnecessary costs (including legacy costs) and inefficient work processes. By following this guide, management can be confident that it did everything possible to support the organization's strategic objectives. At the same time, management's relationship with its union should improve and the resulting CBA is expected to be well received by the union, its members, your supervisors, and your managers.

Who Needs This Guide?

If you are a senior human resources practitioner or an operations manager with labor accountability, or if you are a college student studying human resources management, you need this guide. This is a practical manual to help you achieve better labor agreements through the agility you will develop with improved planning and preparation. There are many courses and books about *how to* negotiate, but I challenge you to find any that teach you *how to plan and prepare* to negotiate.

You wouldn't compete in the Olympics without having first practiced your sport over and over again, or without having a training plan to ensure you are fully prepared as you start competing, or without having coaches who help you think through what strategies to use with the competition. You wouldn't lead soldiers into battle without training them and drilling into them what to do and what not to do in the heat of battle. And you wouldn't play chess without having studied successful openings and alternative responses to unexpected maneuvers. You would plan. You would prepare. You would get yourself ready.

"Plans are worthless, but planning is everything," Dwight Eisenhower said, "[b]ut if you haven't been planning, you can't start to work, intelligently at least."[1] This guide is about how managers should or could be planning for labor agreement negotiations. This guide is not about the negotiation process itself. This is about the work of planning, the work of preparing.

If you were a military strategist, you might take lessons from the last war and make some adjustments to the strategies and tactics that were successful last time. However, if you have studied some of the great military strategists, you understand that while you must consider the past and make basic assumptions about tomorrow on which to build your plans, the actual battle or war or negotiation will unfold differently. Nonetheless you must plan. Remember that old saying that "those who fail to plan, plan to fail." Planning allows you to explore various scenarios and their outcomes. It is a kind of simulation. Done well, it does not lock in your

---

[1] Excerpt from a talk by D.D. Eisenhower. November 14, 1957. *Remarks at the National Defense Executive Reserve Conference.* Transcript by G. Peters and J.T. Woolley, The American Presidency Project, www.presidency.ucsb.edu/node/233951.

thinking or actions. Instead, it can heighten your awareness and speed your recognition of and responses to challenges and opportunities.

Negotiating a CBA or labor agreement is not at all the same as negotiating a business contract with a vendor or service provider. Perhaps the biggest difference is that labor agreement negotiations have a distinct set of legal requirements addressing the process. What other business negotiation includes process steps that are federally mandated? Your executive colleagues who are very experienced with various business negotiations will offer well-intended advice. Be sure to sync up that advice with the legal requirements unique to labor and in keeping with your overarching long-term labor strategy.

Will the Suggestions in This Guide Really Help When It's Time to Bargain?

Aside from learning the legal requirements of the process, you can probably get through the basic negotiations process without formal training or extensive preparation. Some management negotiators follow well-established, trusted routines to prepare. Others review a few cost-sensitive elements with their executive colleagues and then negotiate by the seat of their pants. Others delegate the negotiations voice to an outside party such as a consultant or attorney. Each of these approaches works to an extent, but at what cost? What did you leave on the table? What improvement opportunities did your organization miss because of a failure to prepare thoroughly? How will the process and outcome inform your future labor–management relationship? How will it inform the morale of your employees (the union's members) and your supervisors? Are you fully utilizing this process to further develop your own skills, those of your team, and set the stage for future managers?

This guide takes you through a flexible preparation process and its timing. You decide which elements you and your team will employ. You may choose to pursue every element in this guide or only a handful or something in between. You can customize any element to better fit your organization. You can add elements. This gives you options, which in turn, gives you greater agility. Importantly, it also gives you the timing for each phase, and the why or business reason for each planning element.

This is not a legal guide. This is an offering of process steps to help you prepare. This guide does not guarantee a specific outcome. Instead, it helps you think through how to prepare. This business guide is a hands-on real-world approach to mapping out what could and should be done.

This is not a manual to be followed rigidly step by step. It is a guide, not an algorithm. Work with its ideas and suggestions; mold them to suit your specific needs and timeline. Come back to it as your situation changes. Come back to it again as you start planning subsequent negotiations.

First, take a moment to reflect on the purpose of learning. The deep purpose of learning is to learn how to learn. Framing good questions is often a more important part of the process of problem-solving than memorizing routes to solutions. Questions help drive conversations. Bargaining a new CBA is a kind of conversation. And a conversation is more than the part where you talk and the part where you wait to talk. Active listening is part of any constructive conversation. As you listen, you should consider what adjustments you might need to make to your planned talking points. Agility is so important; it allows you to quickly adjust, adapt, and respond. This guide's suggestions for planning and preparing will help develop your agility muscles, your pivot muscles.

Think about the many stakeholders who have a good reason to want a great outcome from bargaining. Spend time anticipating the future. Anticipate what skills you need to develop in yourself to do better than last time, what skills your current management team needs, what will expected successors need, what legacy will you leave behind that will be impactful to your organization? Remember that the changes memorialized in the upcoming collective bargaining agreement will bind or restrict your organization for many CBAs in the future. Or, these changes can give your successors opportunities to adjust processes and manage costs in ways that ultimately benefit all stakeholders.

Learning to Negotiate a CBA

Think about how you learned to prepare for labor agreement negotiations. If you have already been through the process, there was probably someone at your organization who had their own approach, and you did what they told you to do. That process worked for them and for your organization. Why not follow it? At what frequency did this mentor handle labor negotiations? Once every two or three years? Every four or five years? If they are singularly focused on negotiating CBAs as their primary job function, they might handle several negotiations each year for your organization. Still, how did they learn their process? How are they teaching you? Most likely, it's a kind of apprenticeship approach. That is just one way to prepare for negotiations. It worked in the past. This guide suggests it can be improved.

Contrast your learning experience with your union counterparts. How did they learn? They probably had a similar, but more vigorous apprenticeship approach. And most likely that was supplemented with formal training from their national organization and opportunities to observe a few negotiations. Frankly, their experience at the table is probably stronger than yours. Their regular day-in, day-out work as a union representative includes negotiating labor agreements not just with your organization, but also with all the organizations whose employees are represented by the same union local. For each CBA negotiation you have personally been involved with during the life of your current labor agreement, how many CBAs has this union rep negotiated? I guarantee you it's not one for one. Your union counterparts are likely to have much, much more experience at the table than you do.

How do you mitigate that level of hands-on experience? You do it with good solid, thoughtful preparation. That's key to management's success at the table. Lots of prep, just as you would invest into any big, important management project. Your preparation and planning need to extend beyond just getting this next CBA done. What do you need to put into motion this time to set the stage for the next CBA negotiation and for the next one after that? How can you push the envelope or at the least, nudge the parties in a direction that the organization needs and aligns with the company's long-term strategic vision?

Succession Planning

How can you grow your negotiations managers, move them from good to superior? One way to think about their individual growth needs is to assess each of them against a competency model. One such model was designed for aspiring human resource professionals and can be applied to all negotiations managers including operations managers with labor accountability. The Society of Human Resource Management (SHRM)[2] has identified nine large groupings of competencies—relationship management, ethical practice, HR expertise or knowledge (think labor relations in particular for this discussion), business acumen, critical evaluation, cultural effectiveness, leadership and navigation, consultation, and communication. The model describes key concepts of each competency and offers practical advice for each. Using this model for all your management negotiators gives you the ability to assess and build bench strength not just for the current upcoming negotiation, but for future CBA negotiations as well. It helps you to appropriately place labor negotiations as a critical part of your organization's long-term strategy. Seeing and seizing opportunities and addressing challenges in the heat of the bargaining moment is the goal. You get there by becoming agile. You become agile by giving yourself the time and process to carefully plan and prepare, all of which are on top of your regular full-time work.

What This Book Offers

This guide comes from my 20+ years in labor relations. I've been on management negotiations teams for a variety of businesses, large and small. I've been in negotiations that were traditionally structured and in some that were interest-based. I helped negotiate a contract that was the lead contract in its industry and changed how future wage changes were calculated, not just for our own CBA, but for all the CBAs in a particular industry and region. These CBAs included a "most favored nation"[3] clause. I was on a team that negotiated a multiemployer contract. I helped negotiate a first-time (initial) contract. I held my Senior Professional in Human Resources (SPHR) certification for 20 years and I have a Masters in Labor Relations

---

[2] Information about SHRM's competency model can be found at www.shrm.org.
[3] A "most favored nation" clause in a collective bargaining agreement "allow[s] an employer to obtain from a union the best economic terms for labor among all of the employers that have a collective bargaining relationship with the union within a specified industry or region. If the union subsequently enters into a CBA with a different employer in the identified industry or region that provides for lower-cost wages or benefits, an employer that has negotiated a most favored nation (MFN) clause can demand that its CBA be modified to adopt those more favorable wages and benefits." See www.content.next.westlaw.com (accessed August 22, 2021).

and Human Resources. This guide comes from all these experiences and is offered to managers who want to do the best possible job preparing so they can achieve their organization's desired outcomes. I doubt any other management guide offers you this level of preparation detail or timing considerations.

This guide will help you build muscle memory around how to create proposed new CBA language, how to explain why a particular proposal is beneficial, and how to think about negotiating the best case and acceptable case for your ask. Done well, your preparation will inform potential responses to both expected and unexpected union proposals. In real-time bargaining, you can refer back to management's proposed language that was drafted in calmer times, and move it forward with or without modification. The data analyses and logical arguments will have already been developed. You will be prepared for surprises. By definition, a surprise is something unknown in advance. How do you prepare for it if you didn't expect a particular proposal from the union? That's the paradox. The solution is flexible planning and preparation, which gets you to agility in the moment. And that's what this guide is about.

This guide breaks management's preparation into four distinct phases, mapped out chronologically over time. First is the big picture, high-level strategic-focused planning. Second is the preparation plan, the work plan that will drive your preparation. Third is negotiating the prebargaining agreements, bargaining calendar, and process guidelines, and a bit about negotiations themselves. Fourth is implementing the new CBA.

Most managers facing labor agreement negotiations are looking at doing all this work on top of their already very full-time jobs. Identifying and then prioritizing which elements will be pursued by your team will allow you to create a thoughtful, measured timeline that makes robust preparation more manageable. And more than likely, your team will enjoy better outcomes.

Upward of 17,000[4] labor agreements are negotiated on average, year after year after year. Nearly all CBAs that were in place yesterday will still be in place years into the future. That said, management will be well

---

[4] Federal Mediation and Conciliation Service: www.fmcs.gov/resources/documents-and-data.

served to develop a thoughtful, planned approach to its next labor agreement negotiation and to the one after that and the one after that.

Getting Started

There are two steps you should take right away. First, determine the midpoint date of your current CBA. If you haven't yet arrived at that date, you have plenty of time to do all the work you would like to do. If you are past that date, starting thinking in terms of two buckets of work. One bucket has just those activities you want to focus on for the upcoming negotiation. The other bucket has everything else. "Activities" are simply the elements described in each phase of this guide.

The second step to take right away is to read through this guide, cover to cover, to get an initial impression of the actions suggested in each phase. With your midpoint date in mind, you can quickly assess which items go into which bucket.

PHASE ONE

Plan

Elements or preparation steps for the reader to select from in this chapter are listed in the recommended order of succession. You select the steps you wish to use based on your organization's needs and the context in which you will be bargaining.

Phase One is all about the initial high-level strategic planning and creating a big picture timeline. It's akin to the visioning exercises businesses often do as part of their longer term strategic planning. It includes a kind of SWOT[1] analysis of your labor strategy.

This is the 30,000-foot view of the terrain in front of you. Are there new or higher mountains that need to be accounted for? Is there an active volcano threatening to erupt? Are there new sink holes that you need to maneuver around? Is there a storm brewing? What is the current climate? Are you getting any early signals from the union leadership about how complex this next bargaining might be? This view informs the amount and depth of preparation that needs to be done, and importantly, gives you time to do that work. If you ignore Phase One, you will be in a reactive rather than proactive mode. Let's look at each element of this phase.

Timing

This phase should be underway by about mid-point of your current labor agreement.

Create Your Planning Team

Most of Phase One will be done by you with a small team of colleagues. This is a very small group, probably just three people. If someone holds a

---

[1] A SWOT analysis is a structured way to consider a group's Strengths, Weaknesses, Opportunities, and Threats. See www.en.wikipedia.org for additional discussion.

dual role, you may wish to use just two people. This team should include a very senior operations person, a very senior human resources person, and a senior labor expert. Give a memorable name to this planning team. Consider one that when seen on shared calendars, doesn't reveal the topic. Consider some levity in the name to offset the fact that you will meet frequently. This will push your brain to work in ways that it will resist. Play with names like the Three Musketeers, Three Amigos, Three Bears, Agility (always an ironic concept when dealing with labor), Futurists, Klingons, Good Guys. Maybe do some structured brainstorming for practice, and see what great names you can come up with. The senior labor expert will likely be the one to drive this team, calendar meetings, set agendas, and document as needed. When any of the team members is working on something independently, be sure to make time to update your other team members on the status of that work. All for one and one for all, right?

Strategy

Now is the time to review and refresh your long-term labor strategy. What is the history of the union–management relationship? What is the aspirational vision of the relationship? What is the current state of the relationship? What is needed to close the gap and to move the relationship forward? Be sure to reflect on how the relationship could be impacted if there are changes as to who is holding union positions, everything from their expected chief spokesperson to the stewards at your organization.

Define Success

For management, what does a successful CBA negotiation look like? How will you know it when you see it? Will the chief executive officer (CEO), chief financial officer (CFO), and top operations officers agree? Now is the time to start conversations with key stakeholders about what your success will look like. Keep refining those expectations and check in again before negotiations start. Success is not as simple as just surviving the process and avoiding a strike or lockout. Success should be observable and measurable. Success is forward-looking and should contemplate the next chapter of the union–management relationship.

Consider what success will look like from the union's perspective. While wages, benefits, and working conditions are their three critical elements, what specifically will the union be looking for to declare the negotiation a win for them? What is needed to align the two visions of success? Then reflect on what success will look like from the perspective of the union members? Does that change the alignment vision? Can you get to a shared vision of success?

Also consider the structure of the current CBA. Do you expect the union will want to change its format, resequence the articles, or do some major rewrite? If the senior union leadership is new to this contract, they may want to put their own stamp on the CBA so it better fits their own personal preferences. That will add time to the bargaining process.

Key Stakeholders

Who are they? How frequently do you need to update them and in what detail? The CEO needs to stay informed and be able to ask questions. The CFO probably only needs cost impact information for budgeting and future forecasting. What about other executives, what amount of detail do you really need to share? The more detail you tell them, the more they might want to "help" you even if they have no labor background. At this point in the process, simply identify the key stakeholders and start the conversation with your Phase One planning teammates about downstream considerations. This begins the process of setting their expectations and managing the well-intended offers of assistance and guidance.

Budgets

Two budgets are needed and now is the time to begin building both. The first budget will cover the negotiations process itself. It should include any cost to train the management team negotiators as well as the full cost of the negotiations meeting space and food, plus supplies for negotiations, outside trainers and consultants, and so on. While some expenses may ultimately be negotiated with the union to be shared (such as the cost of the negotiations location), for planning purposes assume all these expenses will be covered by management. You should be able to build this budget by reviewing the expenses from last time and refreshing the numbers to anticipate current costs. It is an estimate. When you build your calendar for the preparation work that is needed, return to this initial budget and allocate costs by fiscal year. If these projected expenses are not already in your existing operating budget, be sure to get them approved by whoever approves your budget. They don't recur year after year. Instead, they are attached to the periodic negotiations process and are sometimes not anticipated by financial planners. Start this first budget now and polish it as you build your detailed work calendars.

The second budget will cover the economics of a new CBA. What cost increases are expected year by year for the expected term of the new contract? What cost increases might result from operational changes? Factor in probable wage increases, medical plan contributions, 401(k)/pension/retirement contribution increases, and so on. Be sure to include legacy costs. A good place to start identifying these numbers is with your organization's finance people who are responsible for future cost projections. Once fully refined, this economics budget will ultimately need to be approved by your organization's CEO or their designee. Be sure these approved projections are kept very confidential and only shared with those accountable for the organization's future cost projections. While it is useful to begin building this second budget now, it will likely not be finalized until shortly before negotiations begin. Start it now so you can speak to it with authority at a high level with your CEO, CFO, and executive colleagues. It will help to build their confidence in your negotiating skills.

Key Management Team Members

Management's chief negotiator and second chair, as well as other key team members should be identified now. Because each management team member already has a very busy full-time job, it's important to start the planning and preparation process earlier than many would expect, and to develop a timeline that allows team members to fit the negotiations work into their existing load.

Your team's chief negotiator and second chair will need to have a solid understanding of the current CBA, a working knowledge of operational issues, a solid understanding of wages and benefits, an understanding of the financial impacts year over year of various negotiations proposals, and a solid understanding of the legal requirements of negotiations including give and take expectations, how to structure proposals and counter-proposals, and how to maintain your current position. The personal attributes or competencies desired in a chief negotiator and second chair include being calm under fire, able to keep emotions (their own and others') under control, and the ability to act when needed. They should exhibit "… a paradoxical ability to be both calm and alert, patient and proactive, creative yet fully grounded."[2] They should be well spoken with a clear style of communication. They should be respected by both sides of the table. And they should be able to tell stories to set context and explain the company's proposals and responses. They should be great listeners and have the ability to read body language of those on both sides of the table. A sense of humor will also help.

Identifying your key team members early in the process allows time for any specialized training that will be helpful. For example, if your organization has been negotiating using traditional distributive bargaining and the parties want to shift to interest-based bargaining (IBB) or to a hybrid of traditional and IBB, your chief negotiator and second chair will need some formal training that includes role playing. Training options might be limited to out-of-town sessions offered just once or twice per year. Getting this additional block of training time added to a manager's already full calendar might be challenging, so plan this in advance.

You should also identify other key players who will be on management's negotiations team or who will provide background support. In addition, identify subject matter experts (SMEs) for each article in the current CBA and the history of the current language. It's likely that the SMEs will only be in the background advising the management team; however, if they are respected and trusted by both sides, you may wish to offer to have them provide a kind of witness testimony during negotiations to help explain or clarify terminology or history, or provide useful

---

[2] M. Wheeler. 2013. *The Art of Negotiation: How to Improvise Agreement in a Chaotic World* (New York, NY: Simon & Schuster), p. 14.

information about options the parties might be considering. Medical plan or other benefit specialists SMEs would be one example.

Succession Planning

The prep work that your team is about to undertake is an excellent opportunity to build bench strength of labor preparation experiences. As you work through candidates for all the management roles identified in the previous section, be sure to think in terms of practical experiences needed for succession planning purposes. What assignments can you give to less experienced people to help them understand the preparation process? Can they be in the room for some of management's strategy discussions? Who would you look to if management's chief negotiator and/or second were to suddenly become unavailable? What experiences or training can you give a backup right now?

If you were to use an outside party to be the voice of management by taking the role of management's chief negotiator, who would you use and at what cost? An attorney who has previously conducted labor negotiations might be one option. Make your selection cautiously as most attorneys do not negotiate labor agreements on a regular basis. Mediation specialists and arbitrators are generally not recommended as they are trained to "split the baby," as the saying goes. A better option would be a consultant specializing in representing management during CBA negotiations.[3]

We used a negotiations consultant for behind the scenes advising when we needed to negotiate an initial contract. There are unique federal rules for first contracts that don't apply to negotiating an existing contract. The consultant's thinking and recommendations consistently aligned closely with our overall strategy and goals. Their advice was so helpful that we continued using them as new or more complex labor matters surfaced.

Anticipate the Union's Team Members

Start with anticipating who the union's chief spokesperson(s) will be and assess their personal motivation. Are they wanting to position themselves

---

[3] Burdzinski & Partners, Inc. has been offering this as one of their primary services for many decades. More information at www.burdzinski.com.

for a different, higher level role in the union organization? If so, what do you think they personally need to accomplish with this next negotiation? Can you trust what they say at negotiations? Consider the relationship between the chief spokesperson and the chief stewards and stewards in the bargaining unit at your organization. Is it good or is it bumpy? What about their relationship with the members? Do the members know and respect the union senior leadership? Do the same with the anticipated second chair for the union.

Think about the chief stewards and stewards at your organization. Are they respected by the members? Are they respected by the chief spokesperson and second? Is there tension, gamesmanship, mutual respect? Is there talk about getting a different union in place? When does the term of office expire for the union's chief spokesperson? If it looks like the timing means they will be campaigning while the parties are negotiating a CBA, consider what you can do proactively to mitigate that situation.

Many full-time union representatives with whom I've interacted have been inconsistent in how they present themselves. A few are consistently difficult to work with, which may well be deliberate. Their stated reasoning is inconsistent. Their stated goal is inconsistent. A very few are fairly open and consistent about their stated goal and the reasons behind it. Many shift with the wind, sometimes being very open and easy to understand, other times being completely inconsistent in their messaging. Many just ignore downstream consequences. Some live for an opportunity to create problems for management, regardless of what their members want.

Who is the real decision maker on the union's team? Who are the influencers with the other union negotiators? Who are the influencers with the members? Is there tension or discontent within the expected union negotiations team? What is the story behind that angst?

Understanding the internal union dynamics and anticipating possible changes will inform your preparation process. Can you trust them when they suggest that the next round of bargaining will be easy and fast? Is everything really that stable? A good understanding of what may be going on within the union ranks will help you be agile from the get-go.

For one negotiation, we expected the union representative for our organization's bargaining unit to be especially unpredictable at the table.

And while he was not the chief negotiator, he was one of the key union reps and his behavior impacted others on his team. One of his goals was to disrupt the union's chief spokesperson. It was part of a longer term strategy of his to challenge the existing union hierarchy so he could ultimately carve out a new role for himself. We worried that he might not be forthcoming when presenting the tentative final agreement to the members for ratification. Ironically, some of our union employees approached us with similar concerns. We encouraged them to speak with the union's chief spokesperson about their issues, and perhaps discuss possibly having employee observers at the table who could then help the union rep present the union's story to the members at their ratification meetings. We later heard that the observers found it necessary to clarify and even correct some of the information the union rep reported at their meetings.

Risks and Mitigation Measures

After just a few sessions with your small planning team, you will have identified several concerns. Start tracking these in a *risk register* that you will keep refining and building on. Begin your mitigation measures right away to achieve the desired outcomes. The risk register can be a simple spreadsheet or Word table that captures the following elements:

- *Risk (and cause)*—Any factor that could interfere with successful completion of your negotiations progress plan.
- *Risk rating*—Combines the probability and severity of impact. Rate the risk "low" if there's a low probability of delaying the progress plan. Rate the risk "medium" if there is a reasonable probability of detrimentally affecting the progress plan. Rate the risk "high" if there's a high probability of delaying the planned progress.
- *Mitigation plan*—This is a simple assessment that for a particular risk the team believes it should "accept," "avoid," or "mitigate" the risk.

Table 1.1 provides some examples.

Table 1.1 Risks and mitigation measures register

Risk (and Cause)	Risk Rating	Mitigation Plan Avoid—Mitigate—Accept
Trust issues: Employees (or supervisors) not trustful of senior management	Medium	Mitigate: Calendar frequent senior managers' informational meetings with work groups to share information and create opportunities for dialog.
Trust issues: Union leadership not aligned with membership	High	Accept
Economics: Union demands may be too high for organization to handle	High	Avoid: Educate union leadership and employees on how the organization makes money and unique business concerns; send out total compensation information to each employee.
Management rights: Degradation of management rights	High	Mitigate: Remind/teach supervisors how to respond with alternate phrases to "because it's management's right."
Strike or threat of strike	Medium	Mitigate: Refresh/expand strike contingency plan; quality of proposed CBA.
Proposed CBA not ratified on first vote	Medium	Mitigate: Identify and address union's assumed top priorities (typically wages).
Union leadership voted out of office after new CBA is ratified	Medium	Accept: Support combined negotiations team with robust communications plan and change plan; focus on quality of contract from employee perspective.

Not long after joining a new organization, I learned that the current term of office for the union's chief spokesperson was going to expire right in the middle of the time window in which we expected to be in labor agreement negotiations. The risk or concern was around how our management negotiators were going to make progress at the table while the rep was campaigning for office. We rated this a high risk, based on issues connected with his election. He would be campaigning for reelection in the midst of bargaining. It was uncertain who his opponent(s) might be and how their campaign might disrupt our bargaining. It quickly became obvious to us that we needed a time separation between the election campaign and our bargaining.

What mitigation measures or options could we as managers pursue? One option was to ask the union to move their election date. The union was unwilling or unable to move the date of the election, so we talked with them about extending the end date of the current contract until well after their election, or starting negotiations early enough to be confident of completing it well before election. Ultimately, we agreed to start negotiations earlier than originally planned. The "only" negative consequence was the reduced window of time for management to prepare for negotiations. This was an acceptable option because we were preparing early. Early preparation gave us agility.

Calendar #1

If you are like me, you will create a few different calendars ranging from simple high-level views to increasingly detailed views. They serve different purposes, different audiences. Some calendars are simply task lists organized in chronological order.

When you create any calendar, be thoughtful about the reasons behind it and who the audience will be. All of the calendars described in this guide need to be customized to show your own organization's activities and available time. Your first calendar will probably be very high level, with the timeline called out in broad strokes, perhaps using quarters of the calendar year rather than months or days.

If you are giving a 30,000-foot briefing to managers and supervisors who really don't need details, consider something as simple as Table 1.2.

While intentionally obscure, it gives a sense of the flow and general timing. It signals that you have a plan and that they don't need to jump in to help you. It keeps them informed enough to not worry. Remember how important communication is in this process, but also remember to adjust the communication details for the audience with whom you are engaged.

Table 1.2 Calendar #1: Focus on phases

Phase	Time →
Phase 1: Plan	⟶
Phase 2: Prepare	⟶
Phase 3: Negotiate	⟶
Phase 4: Implement	⟶

On the other hand, if you are speaking with executives or members of management's negotiations team, you might want to use a different type of high-level calendar such as the one shown in Table 1.3. Instead of showing phases of work, list a few sample activities including the strike contingency plan; include a general sense of timing by showing the start and end time for each activity relative to other sample activities.

Table 1.3 Calendar #2: Focus on activities

Activity	Time →
Identify management and expected union priorities	
Establish budget	
Identify training needs and select trainer(s)	
Conduct training	
Review and update strike contingency plan	
Select negotiations facility and organize logistics	
Conduct negotiations	

It's important to note that the activities and timing of this calendar do not necessarily sync up with earlier or later calendar examples. Each calendar needs to be customized to reflect the work of your specific CBA planning and preparation effort. These examples are intended to guide your thinking, not dictate which activities you might choose or the amount of time you will spend on each.

Brainstorming Sessions (Part One)

Reach out to supervisors and higher to identify things that seem to be limited by the current CBA or by the current practice. What is not working? What could be better? These should be confidential brainstorming sessions. Manager/supervisor meetings should be held to solicit ideas. These meetings might need to be facilitated by executives to get the supervisors to safely open up. As with any true brainstorming process, ideas should not be discarded out of hand. Instead, they should be welcomed and captured on a master brainstorming list that will begin your *wish list* (management's list of possible changes to the CBA). Wish lists as well as refining and filtering these ideas will be discussed further in Phase Two.

Instead of relying exclusively on face-to-face brainstorming sessions, you might consider first surveying the supervisors and managers. As shown in Table 1.4, for each article in the CBA, ask them to rate the difficulty or inefficiency in their daily operations by scoring the article as "no difficulty," "minor or acceptable level of difficulty," or "major or frequent difficulty." This might be an initial filter for structuring subsequent face-to-face conversations with small groups of supervisors. It's important to give supervisors and managers the opportunity to voice their concerns and ensure they are being heard, so don't use surveys as a substitute for that important interaction.

Table 1.4 Scorecard of current CBA difficulties

	Article Name	No Difficulty	Minor or Acceptable Level of Difficulty	Major or Frequent Difficulty
1	Guarantees	X		
2	General Provisions	X		
3	Seniority		X	
4	Selection and Assignment		X	
5	Working Conditions			X
...	(continue with all CBA articles)			

Training

Labor agreement negotiations are different from other types of contract negotiations. They involve careful balancing of multiple pressures—staying within the prescribed labor laws for CBA negotiations (required back-and-forth discussions, required give and take of proposals, frequency of formal talks, and more), working to improve the relationship of the parties, supporting the organization's short- and long-term business priorities, and helping the union understand how to "sell" the proposed CBA changes to its members when it's time to ratify the tentatively agreed to contract. Not every member of management's negotiations team needs to be an expert in all of this, but certainly the chief spokesperson and second chair must know who to turn to at what point. And they must know which phrases to use in certain situations and which phrases to absolutely avoid. An inadvertent misstep at the bargaining table can, at a minimum, provoke a dramatic outburst from your union counterpart, which is usually intended to be a show for their union colleagues rather than true anger at your action. A misstep might cause a world of frustration with your executive colleagues, for example, if you unwittingly give the union the right to review your organization's otherwise confidential financial records.

Most of the traditional bargaining I've participated in involved at least one instance of the union chief spokesperson slapping the table, loudly declaring that they've had enough, and storming out of the meeting room. I suspect it may be part of the union's training.

I coached one management team to turn the tables during an unusual bargaining session. We had been having a difficult series of conversations about wages with no real progress, so in our management caucus I encouraged our management leadership to let their frustration show and to do so as dramatically as they could. Our second chair was a former college football player. When we reconvened talks with the union, our former football player stayed seated while he talked, but appeared to grow physically larger as he spoke. He leaned forward with intensity. He made his body as big as he could while sitting down, but kept his voice steady as he informed the union that he was fed up and was ready to walk away.

Management's chief spokesperson then said that she was personally insulted that the union had been wasting everyone's time with alternative proposals that were illogical and impossible to implement. Another management senior leader tapped into her high school drama class training, allowed her voice to shake and tears to well up as she shared her own frustration. Members of the union's team began to individually apologize and several were clearly emotionally distraught realizing that they had overstepped. With that our former football player colleague stood up and informed the union that they could find us in our caucus room when they were ready to really negotiate. Then our management team walked out. The union rep stopped by hours later, congratulated us on our move, saying he didn't think we had it in us. Our next session saw meaningful progress. Our message to the employees on the union's negotiations team had been received.

Develop an initial plan and approximate timeline for training management negotiators. Remember that some training is only offered once or twice per year, which means calendars and budgets need to be considered. Include some basic training on the negotiations process, including the legal requirement to change positions. Consider whether any team members might benefit from some training on emotional intelligence, reading nonverbal (body) language, or similar soft skills that could improve their performance during negotiations. A simple listing of who needs to be trained on what will be helpful. Add the training dates to your next calendar and onto the calendars of those who need training.

If the parties agree in advance to use interest-based bargaining (IBB) or a hybrid of IBB and traditional bargaining, additional steps will be needed. Very early in the planning process, gain the union's formal agreement to use IBB, agree on who will deliver the process training to both parties together, and how the training cost will be assigned (shared or assigned entirely to management). Be sure to document the agreement with both parties signing. Consider joint training for both negotiating teams about divergent personalities. The *Myers–Briggs Type Indicator* and *Thomas Kilmann Conflict Mode Instrument*[4] might be useful considerations although their popularity has been dropping recently. Recommended readings such as *Getting to Yes*[5] might also be helpful.

---

[4] The *Myers–Briggs Type Indicator* (MBTI) is available through CPP, Inc., www .cpp.com. It identifies 16 different personality types to describe people. Standard language in its interpretive reports suggests that, "A clear understanding of the basics of personality type and type development will help you gain greater understanding of yourself and others and the impact type has on daily interactions." The *Thomas Kilmann Conflict Mode Instrument* (TKI) is available through CPP, Inc., www.cpp.com. It assesses an individual's behavior in conflict situations, and describes a person's behavior along two basic dimensions: (1) assertiveness and (2) cooperativeness. Five different methods for dealing with conflict are identified. Guidance is provided for when and how to use each method based on an individual's own profile.

[5] R. Fisher and W. Ury. 1981. *Getting to Yes: Negotiating Agreement Without Giving In* (New York, NY: Penguin Books).

If the parties plan to use traditional bargaining, be sure that the key management negotiators, if not the entire management negotiations team, get some formal training that includes role playing and a discussion of the legal expectations of the CBA bargaining process.[6] Capture the training and dates on your next calendar and ensure the person to be trained calendars the training as well.

Physical and Mental Health

Speak candidly with your management team members to encourage them to individually consider what small changes they might make to help them handle a prolonged period of stress. Exercising regularly, reducing caffeine and alcohol, eating more of the right things and less of the wrong things, doing yoga and/or meditating are all sound ideas. Consider advice that has been developed over the years to address combat fatigue. The similarities are striking.

Bargaining Location

You can start researching locations yourself and use your research to inform your later conversations with your union counterpart since the final decision is something that must be negotiated. Options usually include your organization's in-house conference rooms, the union's in-house conference rooms, meeting space in a hotel, and executive conference space in a convention hotel. Let's consider each option.

- *Your organization's in-house conference rooms.* On the plus side, this option is very affordable since presumably there is no out-of-pocket expense to use the company's own in-house conference rooms. Two concerns surface immediately. First is around the impact to other employees

---

[6] One such program is Michigan State University's *Negotiating Labor Management Agreements for Competitive Advantage*, which focuses on traditional bargaining. Sessions are offered jointly to both union and management attendees. More information at hrlr.msu.edu/hr_executive_education/programs /negotiating_labor_management_agreements.

who might need the conference rooms. Is there sufficient other space available for them? Second is that management's negotiators will likely wander away to their own individual offices or to chase down some piece of business, thereby distracting them from the negotiations work and risking fueling the gossip mill.

- *The union's in-house conference rooms.* With good reason, there is an urban legend that at least some unions install listening devices in their in-house conference rooms. Why risk allowing the union to eavesdrop on your private conversations? The union will suggest that there's no cost for their meeting space and that each party can take turns bringing in donuts and pizza. The time and effort needed to plan and order food and beverages each day is not something you want the management negotiations team to take on. Better to keep them focused on bargaining and their regular "day job" work.

- *Meeting space in a hotel.* This is often preferred especially if you can arrange for separate caucus rooms for the management and union teams. Some hotels will temporarily convert standard sleeping rooms into meeting rooms, making that their option for your caucus rooms. Ensure that you can use the hotel's meeting room(s) late into the evening if you need to. Oftentimes, hotels will book evening events starting at 6:00 p.m. or later, meaning you will need to finish well before then so the hotel staff can clean up from your meeting and reset the tables and chairs for the evening's event. Hotels expect to make more money providing food and beverages than charging rent for meeting room space, and they may charge you a fee for bringing in your own food and beverages. In this arrangement the hotel will charge you a set rate for the meeting room(s), and will try to make most of its money on the food and beverage arrangements. You may be able to level set the playing field by agreeing in advance to a set menu with limited variations. Hotels usually prefer to settle room rentals on a daily basis, but you may be able to arrange for weekly billing or in some cases, monthly billing if there are guarantees in place.

- *Executive conference space in a convention hotel setting.*
  This could be ideal for your negotiations. Typically, it's a separate wing of a large hotel and is dedicated to business meetings. You would likely need one large meeting room to accommodate the full negotiations team, plus two smaller rooms to be used for separate union and management caucus sessions. Food and beverage arrangements may be negotiable as to the offerings and pricing. Printing and photocopy services may be included for no additional charge. Pricing for the total package will likely be on a per person per day basis and you'll have more luck with price considerations if you can guarantee a certain number of days with a minimum participant count guarantee. The hotel will probably be comfortable with weekly or monthly billing. This is my preferred option as it can all be negotiated with the hotel well in advance of the actual negotiations.

Experiences and locations can vary considerably. My very first experience at the table was for a multiemployer CBA. This one agreement covered multiple small independent companies in the same industry and multiple union locals from the same national union. There were close to 20 people on each side of the table and we met in hotel meeting rooms (usually a large private dining room) all over the state to be respectful of the vast geographic region represented in the contract. Caucus rooms were nonexistent, so each side had stand-up meetings in the hallway or outside by the hotel pool. It was not conducive to good progress. My second CBA negotiation was the polar opposite. Three people for management and two for the union, and it was all finished in a few half-day sessions, all of which were held in the company's board room. Plan ahead in order to secure the space you want.

Your consideration of negotiation locations in Phase One should focus on brainstorming a list of options suitable for the current bargaining expectations. In Phase Two you will work with your union counterpart to decide on the location and determine what, if any, cost sharing there will be.

External Economic Data

Be sure you have updated data about your local market. The consumer price index (CPI) is referenced in many CBAs and often cited by union negotiators at the table. Cost-of-living adjustments (COLAs) and reopeners are often based on changes to the CPI. If your organization's employee turnover rate is average to high, you should be knowledgeable about the local unemployment rate for key union positions. And you should be conversant about best practices and trends within your industry. Consider surveying other unionized organizations in your industry to understand their most recent changes in wages and benefits in particular. Assume the union will have done this.

Employee Demographic Data

Ask your internal compensation and benefits team to start looking at the demographics of the union population covered by your CBA. For example, is there a high percentage of employees who are eligible for retirement? If so, you may need time to consider whether to offer an incentive package to encourage voluntary retirements. If you choose to explore this path, consider how many people at one time would be manageable? Make time to review the numbers needed for each type of job and location so you can anticipate your recruiting needs. Study the demographics to determine what patterns emerge that may need addressing.

Historical Financial Review

If you don't already maintain a running list of historical pay changes and such, ask your internal financial analysts to create one for you, starting with the oldest CBA you have on file and noting every pay rate change since then. It's useful to note not only wage changes but also changes such as supplemental pay, pension benefits, health care coverage, and paid time off (PTO). This will be a useful resource for when the management teams develop their white papers (in Phase Two) and again when economics are discussed at the table (in Phase Three). Be sure this list is updated shortly before the start of bargaining.

Lessons Learned (Part One)

Start logging *lessons learned* as you work through the different phases of planning and preparing to negotiate. Add to it in each Phase including the Implement Phase. This will help reveal gaps in your strategy and tactics, and will help refine your process for future bargaining sessions.

Notice of Bargaining

Be sure the *Notice of Bargaining Form F-7* has been submitted to the Federal Mediation and Conciliation Service (FMCS). This is a very simple form that informs the other side that it wishes to discuss a change to the current CBA. It also notifies the FMCS that their mediation help might be needed if negotiations stall.

For private sector organizations, the F-7 is to be filed with the other party at least 60 days prior to the start of negotiations. Health care organizations must file at least 90 days prior. Usually, the union will be the party to file the F-7 since they are the ones who most often wish to change something even if it is to only negotiate wage increases for the next few years. Assuming the union files the F-7, there is no need for the employer to also submit an F-7. The FMCS will assign an officer who will periodically reach out separately to the union and to management to confirm that progress is being made.

There's a technical argument that if the F-7 form is not filed by the union, you don't need to meet with them to bargain a new contract. You would be in for an interesting debate if the current CBA expires before a new CBA is in place, and if there is no formal agreement to operate under an extension of the current CBA. I've chosen to discretely remind the union that they needed to file rather than engage in that debate. While it can be satisfying to put the union leadership in an awkward position, that position would ultimately impact their members, your employees, and the bargaining climate, so why do it?

Why does this early planning work of Phase One matter? It sets the stage accurately, warts and all. It informs downstream activities such as specialized training that often have timing and availability limitations. It informs key stakeholders who might otherwise be tempted to second guess your work or look over your shoulder. It provides you and your management team with a methodical and manageable approach to prepare for negotiations on top of other daily work. It is a road map of what needs to happen next. And it gives you the time to map out the work so you and your team can get it done on top of your other work.

As you wrap up Phase One, be sure to create documents that are useful for you and your colleagues. There is a lot of information to track and to communicate with various stakeholders. And now you are ready to move into the heavy lift phase. All hands, on deck!

PHASE TWO

Prepare

Elements or preparation steps for the reader to select from in this chapter are listed in the recommended order of succession. You select the steps you wish to use based on your organization's needs and the context in which you will be bargaining.

Phase Two is the detailed preparation, similar to the in-the-weeds work that you would do for other big projects. Whereas Phase One is the 30,000-foot view of the terrain ahead, Phase Two is all about specifics. How dense is the forest? What kind of trees? Are there desserts or cacti along the way? Any rivers and creeks that may need to be crossed? Are the bridges in good working condition? What are the expected seasonal factors? Rain, snow, fog, sandstorms, fire danger? Think in terms of the features that the troops on the ground will need to navigate. These are the particulars that the management negotiations team will need when they bargain a new CBA in real time.

This is the big lift in the prenegotiations work. This builds on the strategies and analyses that you and the Three Musketeers developed in Phase One. You will identify the specifics of the work to be done, by whom, and in what timeframe. There will be dependencies in some instances, meaning some work will have to be done before other work can be done. One informs the other. By nature, I'm a list maker, an organizer of stuff, so this is fun for me. I recognize that some people find fun in other ways. Welcome to my world.

Timing

This is the longest duration of the four phases. It should begin before Phase One is fully complete, and will still be in process when Phase Three begins. Overlap is not a bad thing here. If you do not perform the critical Phase Two work, you put your organization at risk for not achieving the best possible outcome at contract negotiations. Performing this work prepares your team with the arguments it needs at the table and with the emotional strength to stay calm. It guides you through a robust analysis of the various points in the contract that are not going well and helps you develop responses to anticipated union points of concern. It gives you the agility to pivot. The in-depth strike planning process will give your team the confidence that even if bargaining were to shut down, the management team can continue to conduct the work of the business with minimal disruption. This level of confidence makes the team much stronger at the table. We are prepared, it says, for everything. We are prepared to fight if need be. We are a team, we are ready. *Je suit prêt.*[1]

Confidentiality

And to state what should be obvious, all the work that you and your colleagues do or even think about doing to prepare for negotiations is absolutely confidential. There should be no sharing of any kind of information with anyone who is not on the team. Be super cautious around supervisors who are directing the daily work of union employees. You do not want to put them in an awkward position, so if they ask, simply confirm that there is some work being done but no details are being shared outside the room, period. End of discussion. Be firm.

Calendar #3

As a segue into Phase Two, start building your next calendar. Capture the critical details and dates from your Phase One high-level planning, and start organizing the work ahead. Table 2.1 shows examples. The primary audience for this calendar is management's negotiations team, both the people who expect to be at the table and the people who will be providing support. They need to understand your timeline for the work ahead.

---

[1] *Je suit prêt* is French for "I am ready." It is the clan motto of the Frasers of Scotland, made famous in the recent *Outlander* books (by author Diana Gabaldon) and television series. Outlander's 18th century spelling reads, *Je suit prest.*

Table 2.1 Calendar #3: Representative activities by phase

Representative Activities by Phase	Time →
Phase One: Plan	
Develop/refresh strategy	→
Define success	→
Identify key stakeholders	→
Develop budgets	——————→
Identify key management team	→
Anticipate union's team	→
Track risks and mitigations	———————→
Develop calendar #1	→
Hold brainstorming sessions	→
Phase Two: Prepare	
Create calendar #2	→
Develop and vet white papers	——————→
Plan strike contingency	——————→
Phase Three: Negotiate	
Select facility	→
Develop negotiations schedule	→
Develop rules for bargaining	→
Conduct collective bargaining	→
Ratify proposed contract	→
Phase Four: Implement	

Important: Remember that the activities and timing of this calendar do not necessarily sync up with earlier or later calendar examples. Each calendar needs to be customized to reflect the work of your own planning and preparation effort. These examples are intended to guide your thinking, not dictate which activities you might choose or the amount of time you will spend on each.

Do not fall into the trap of focusing only on bargaining. You will be more confident and more successful if you plan and prepare fully, consistent with the suggestions in this guide.

Review Prior Bargaining Notes

Return to the *lessons learned* notes from your organization's prior negotiations and keep that information in mind as you develop your plans. Study the *daily moves* document (from your last round of bargaining) that summarizes the number of counter-proposals and support reasons for each CBA article during the last CBA negotiation. What patterns emerge? What if management's negotiations team did not create a *daily moves* document last time? Create it now by reviewing negotiations notes and capturing the dates of both sides' initial proposals and counter-proposals, along with the dates of proposals that were tentatively agreed to at the table.

Total Compensation Statements

Plan to develop total compensation statements and schedule their distribution to employees to occur shortly before bargaining begins. In addition to direct compensation such as base pay and incentive pay, include details of indirect compensation such as the employer portion of health, dental, and vision plans, flexible spending accounts, retirement and 401(k) contributions, paid leave programs including vacation/sick time/ PTO as well as holiday, personal time off, bereavement leave, military leave, and jury duty. Also include disability insurance and life insurance, employee assistance program, relocation expenses, tuition assistance and learning and development offerings, and so on. Issuing these statements shortly before bargaining begins is an effective way for organizations to message how well employees are already compensated.

Review Documents for the Current CBA Period

Review grievances, disciplines, and attendance for the term of the contract that is about to expire. If you don't already have ongoing lists for each of these categories of concern, develop them and start looking for patterns that you or the union might want to discuss in negotiations. Are there articles or sections of the current CBA that are problematic or have been cited frequently in grievances, for example? What about differences between the parties around intent of the current language? Be sure to review any mediation and arbitration settlements as well as memoranda of agreement for commitments to continuing a practice under a new CBA or otherwise suggesting a need to discuss at the table. Experienced negotiators often focus on the same issues in each of their negotiations. Look for patterns.

What is a pattern? A wise professor explained to me that if something happens once, it is an anomaly. If it happens twice, it's a coincidence. When it happens three times, it's a pattern. But three times out of how many instances? Three for three might be meaningful, but three out of one hundred may not be so. Regardless of whether the pattern is important from management's perspective, it could be very important from the union's perspective. Developing these lists and looking for patterns allows you to base your bargaining talking points on actual data. You can respond quickly and calmly, with agility even, and not get drawn into an emotional or protracted debate.

You should be collecting current comparator CBAs. Which unionized organizations do you get union employees from or lose them to? Those are your comparators. The union might have some additional contracts that they like as a reference point for your contract, so if you know what those organizations are, get those CBAs as well in order to understand the union's perspective. Often your compensation specialists will know their counterparts at these other organizations so they can obtain these CBAs for you. Downstream when you are working on the preagreements just prior to the formal start of bargaining, work with the union leadership to determine which comparator contracts the parties will recognize, if any. Specify if the comparators are only for wage discussion or if there is other application intended as well. Be careful not to unwittingly abdicate your organization's needs to a different organization's contract terms.

Start looking at compensation surveys and benefits surveys, and even conducting your own to assess how your organization lines up with your comparators. Is it your organization's intent to be at the midpoint, lead the pack, or something else? In the ideal world, your compensation and benefits strategies would align with your recruitment and retention strategy as well as with your labor and employee relations strategy.[2] For example, if you plan to retain employees for much if not all of their work life, compensation and benefits should motivate people to stay, and your labor relations should work hard to be considerate, respectful, and inclusive of union members' input on implementing changes. On the other hand, if you are comfortable having employees leave after a relatively short tenure with your organization, the pay and benefits do not have to be so generous, and the labor relations might be more assertive, less diplomatic.

Language Clarification

Some managers have been keeping notes about language that wasn't written as clearly as the parties intended and which just needs clarification to better align with practice. And someone has been looking at typos in the CBA document that are simple fixes. Capture these notes in a list called *language clarification*. Add these to your *wish list* (your list of possible proposals for bargaining) so you don't lose track of them. Be sure to include them when management offers its proposed changes to the contract during negotiations.

Brainstorming Sessions (Part Two)

In Phase One you held brainstorming sessions with supervisors to hear their thoughts about what is not working with the current CBA or with the current practice. Now you should take those unfiltered ideas and do some more brainstorming with their managers. Encourage the managers

---

[2] One way to check alignment is to use the "McKensey 7S" model to assess how key elements of your organization work together. Developed in the 1970s by Tom Peters and Robert Waterman, the 7Ss refer to Strategy, Structure, Systems, Shared Values, Skills, Style, and Staff. The idea is that these elements need to be in alignment for the organization to be successful. More information at www .MindTools.com.

and executives to offer additional ideas and then begin the process of refining the ideas. Brainstorm what topics the union will likely bring forward and how critical they might be to the union. If the same thought is worded in two or three different ways, just combine them for now and let the idea be a bit messy. Identify whether the concern is truly an issue with the CBA language or whether it is simply a past practice. If it's CBA language, identify the language including the CBA article and section on your wish list. It could involve multiple sections; if so, list all of them on your wish list.

Your wish list is the best way of tracking all of the suggestions from the initial brainstorming sessions and then managing through the filtering process. If you use an Excel spreadsheet to track from the beginning, you can easily copy the initial list to a new sheet, filter, add notes, and so on. Create a new sheet each time you apply new filters, all in one master document.

If the suggestion is simply a past practice issue, move that to a parking lot list and discuss next steps and timing in a separate meeting. Keep the wish list discussion focused on any CBA language that is limiting or causes problems or keeps the organization from operating as efficiently or as effectively as it might. You can keep track of the language clarification topics and anticipated union topics on the same wish list, just identify the concern as language clarification or an anticipated union ask, as appropriate.

White Papers

White papers are simply very structured position papers, one per topic, that each identify a concern or problem, the current CBA language that is connected with the problem, the history of the language, and management's ideal and acceptable CBA language change(s) that would be needed to resolve the problem.

Depending on the size of your organization, you might want to break into two teams to develop the white papers. One team focuses on operational issues. A second team focuses on human resources issues such as wages, wage structure, benefits offerings, and job moves. Whether you use one team or two, the next step is to refine the wording of the concern so that you have a clear and concise statement of the problem to be solved.

Assign two to three people per topic. For succession planning purposes, populate teams with a combination of bargaining table people and support people who need exposure to CBA bargaining. Consider operations managers, experienced supervisors, and HR specialists.

There should be a separate paper per topic. If there are linkages between topics, make a note to that effect. Everyone should use the same template or outline structure for developing their white papers. And just like we were taught in school, plan the paper before you write it. The template for the outline or plan for the paper might look like the one shown in Table 2.2.

Table 2.2 Confidential white paper outline

Topic	Brief headline or descriptive reference
CBA citation	Article(s) and section(s); also list connected article(s) and section(s)
Problem or concern	This is the refined problem statement from the brainstorming work
Solution	In general terms, what needs to be negotiated to resolve the problem? Be sure this explains why the change is needed; that is, what is the intent? Describe both what you want what to have changed and what you don't want to happen.
Data and analysis	What data needs to be collected to support management's position? What surveys are needed? What is the industry's best practice? What analysis needs to be done? What is the history of this CBA language? When did the language first appear in the CBA? Did it change over the years; if so, why?
Cost impact	Estimate any cost burden or cost savings associated with the proposed change. Be sure to project these estimates forward for the expected term of the new CBA.
Management's SME(s)	Who on the negotiations team knows this topic inside and out? Who on management's negotiations support team can help?
Cultural impact	How will this proposed change be received by the employees and their supervisors? What needs to occur to implement the change beyond informing them? Is specialized training needed? Is a transition period needed?
Union's expected position	What do you anticipate the union's response will be? Will they be amenable to management's proposal or actively resist or something in between? Why?
Proposed CBA language	Draft the new language with specific redlined edits to the current CBA language you recommend to solve the problem. Write language that reflects (a) management's best-case scenario and (b) management's minimal acceptable scenario. Consider whether there is language elsewhere in the CBA that must also be changed for each scenario. Draft that language as well.

It's useful to reconvene the team and discuss each other's outlines before moving on to researching and writing the white papers. This type of constructive feedback is very helpful in terms of scoping the research that need to be done and identifying the language that needs to be addressed.

Writing white papers is one of the biggest and most important steps in preparing for negotiations and it's hard to do. Most of us haven't written a research paper since school, and now we are asking ourselves and our colleagues to do just that. This is a step that is often done poorly, incompletely, or not at all by many management negotiators, yet it is vital for flushing out the problem that needs to be addressed, quantifying it, developing pro and con arguments, developing alternate positions, and drafting possible changes to CBA language. The work done in preparing these papers is key to ensuring agility at the bargaining table.

The outline that you vetted in the brainstorming sessions is the roadmap for the work needed for each paper. Get some trusted support people who need exposure to negotiations and have them help gather data, conduct surveys, and do other research for you. Remind them to respect confidentiality. Encourage the white paper authors to stick with their outlines and provide a clear description for each element of their outline. Some papers might be short, perhaps just a couple of pages. Other papers may be rather lengthy, 10 or more pages, plus attachments showing support data or survey analyses. If contract language for a given provision has changed over the years, review past CBAs and talk with your SMEs to understand why the change was made. Capture the earlier language from prior CBAs and put that in an appendix to the white paper. Force yourself to anticipate multiple paths to reaching your most critical objective with the proposal. The more you think through the union's expected proposal(s) on a given element and your counter-proposals, the better you will be during bargaining. You will have refined the focus of the proposed change and, to reach agreement, you might find that you can accept some amount of accompanying noise that is not your preference. This, too, helps your agility.

Assign a facilitator to ensure progress is made and roadblocks are removed. Some papers will be fairly fast to research and write; others will require a good amount of research. Many papers will need additional work after the team reviews them and provides constructive feedback so stay on top of your timeline for these papers.

Be sure to also develop papers on topics that you anticipate the union will bring forward. Conduct the same level of research on these proposals that you are doing with management's topics. Develop language that management might live with that you can use as a counter-proposal to successfully refute a union-suggested change that management does not wish to accept on surface. Use the same template to outline your research plan and develop your white papers on these expected union topics.

Once the papers have all been pretty well vetted, the team can assign realistic priorities. This can go fairly quickly if you limit the options to "must have," "nice to have," and "not worth a fight." Your high-level Three Musketeers team can further prioritize the top three to five "must have" items for management. Do the same for the expected union topics. These need to be clear in your minds before you come to the table. Having all of this work done in advance gives you and your team the very real opportunity to fully think through last minute changes or adjustments to strategy and priorities. Importantly, you will be able to quickly and confidently map out counter-proposals while you are at the table. Here is where agility pays off.

This is the key preparation step that will diffuse emotions on the management side, and allow you to focus on the required give and take of labor negotiations. Ultimately, these papers should guide you to the best possible outcome. Remember, these papers are only for management to use. They will not be provided to the union, although the data collected or survey results could be shared in support of management's proposals.

Strike Contingency Plan

There are three ways that a *work stoppage* might happen—a legal strike, a wildcat strike, or a lockout. The most common work stoppage is a strike, which is when union employees refuse to work. A *legal strike* is one that complies with all legal and CBA provisions, and is properly approved by the union and the union membership. A *wildcat strike* is an unauthorized strike. It does not comply with legal and/or CBA provisions nor has it been properly approved. It is simply a group of union employees who decide on their own to withhold their labor. A wildcat strike is against the law.[3] A third way a work stoppage might happen is if management determines to block the union employees from reporting to work. This is called a *lockout*. It doesn't happen often but it does happen. For preparation purposes, our strike contingency plan will apply to all three types of work stoppages.

Note that the strike contingency plan should not be widely communicated. Strike planning is extremely important, but for morale purposes, you will want to shield the work from union employees and their immediate supervisors who often trade information.

Strike contingency plans are challenging documents to create and to refresh. This work can be assigned to managers and senior independent contributors who are respected by their colleagues and who can keep their work highly confidential. This is an incredibly important step in preparing for negotiations even if you believe there isn't a snowball's chance that a stoppage will ever happen. On an emotional level, your management team's quiet confidence at the table will rival Clint Eastwood in his Italian westerns or better yet in his *Dirty Harry* movies. "Go ahead, make my day," right?[4] Instinctively your team will know if things do go south at the table, the organization will be positioned to manage the business through a strike the best way it can be done.

I was part of management's negotiations team for an important manufacturing site of a Fortune 250 company. As we were working through our operational priorities, corporate informed us that it was of critical importance to the company that we get random drug testing into our next CBA. Ours would be the first contract in the company to achieve that and it would send an important signal to all our other unionized plants. Their message was that this was a "must have" item, that it would be assigned a higher priority ahead of any operational issue at the plant,

---

[3] The union leadership will probably try to stop a wildcat strike. Because it is not authorized by the union and is against the law, they will not want to be associated with it nor with any bad acts connected with it.

[4] Early in the movie *Sudden Impact* (1984), Clint Eastwood's character, Harry Callahan, stares down an armed robber who is holding a hostage, and dares the robber to give him a reason to shoot him, uttering the famous phrase, "Go ahead. Make my day."

and that we should anticipate that the union we were facing, one of the biggest, "baddest" unions in the country, would strongly resist and that they would likely strike over this one issue.

Every week our small site management team met to work on our topics. And in a separate meeting every week, this same team met to work on our strike contingency plan. The management team anticipated driving through hostile picket lines as soon as the strike began and planned on being locked inside the facility for a minimum of two weeks. To this day, I can tell you when we anticipated the portable washing machines would arrive and how they would be snuck past angry picketers, and I can tell you which interior office I would sleep in since my own office was on the first floor and had exterior windows. To the mattresses![5] We were prepared. *Je suit prêt.* My colleagues and I were calm and confident.

There's more to the story. Several months before our two-week negotiation period began, the corporate head of security and two of his lieutenants were in the local coffee shop getting out of the latest snowstorm of the winter. They were all big, physically strong men. The union's chief negotiator happened to be in the same coffee shop, recognized them, and asked them what they were doing in town. "Looking at fishing locations," was the response from the head of security. "In February?" the union negotiator asked.

Fast forward to the last couple of days of negotiations. The contract was due to expire Saturday night at midnight. Our manager responsible for obtaining the vans we would use to drive into the plant had to pick up the vans on Friday because the car rental office was closed on weekends. He parked the vans at the back of the parking lot of an adjacent business. By sheer luck, late Friday afternoon the chief negotiator for the union happened to drive down the road in front of our plant and just happened to look left in the split second his vehicle passed by that adjacent property. He registered that there were multiple rental vans parked at the back where no vehicles ever parked and he put two and two together.

---

[5] In the movie *The Godfather* (1972), a trusted associate of Vito Corleone observes that Santino (Sonny) Corleone is expecting a protracted war against the other families, saying "That Sonny's running wild. He's thinking about going to the mattresses already. We gotta find a spot over on the West Side."

Corporate security in town scouting out fishing locations in February plus rental vans next door today equals strike prep!

In that instant, he realized that we were willing to take a strike over random drug testing. The union had achieved all the priority items it wanted in negotiations and had simply not prepared for a strike. Now it was too late for them to prepare. By noon Saturday, the parties had agreed to both the concept of random drug testing and to many pages of detailed process language that would be in the new CBA. Go ahead, make my day.

Check your current CBA. Does it contain unambiguous "no strike" language? Does the language address the timing of when a strike may occur? What happens if the new CBA is not ratified before the current CBA expires? Does that increase the possibility of a strike?

Do some research on strikes including the average duration of a strike in your industry in the last 10 years or so.[6] Check the strike history of your part of the country. Check into the strike history of the union with whom you will negotiate. Check your union's local and national websites for information about their strikes and who may authorize a particular strike. I like to get raw historical data from the Bureau of Labor Statistics, then filter it for my industry and separately for the union I'll be bargaining with. It won't prevent a strike, but it will help you understand the probability.

Strikes are usually low probability, high-risk scenarios. You absolutely must prepare a strike plan. If your organization already has a strike plan, refresh it for today. If no strike plan exists, check to see if your organization has an emergency operations plan addressing how different departments will be run (or not run) if there is a natural disaster such as a tornado or earthquake, or if there is a pandemic. If your organization has such a document that is current, it will be a great place to start. Each section needs to be refreshed with a strike scenario in mind, of course. In all instances, the team working on this should have good senior representation from each major operational and administrative department. Be sure to involve your legal team and communications team to understand

---

[6] The U.S. Bureau of Labor Statistics is a great resource for data on work stoppages. More information at www.bls.gov, then click on WSP (Work Stoppage Program). The Federal Mediation and Conciliation Service also has useful data. More information at www.fmcs.gov, then select Resources, then Documents and Data.

when they need to be alerted that a strike is likely or imminent. Remind everyone to respect strict confidentiality.

If your organization has no prior strike plan and no emergency operations plan, you need to allow more time for this step of the process. Begin by gathering your key senior people together. Create a list of basic assumptions. One assumption is around the possible duration of a strike. Plan a two-day scenario, a two-week scenario, and a two-month scenario. Ask each critical operations manager what absolutely must be done in each time window and what can be delayed. Identify how that work will be performed without union employees. Think in terms of required tasks instead of whole jobs. Then consider facility access with your in-house security people. How do you best manage that to minimize disruption? Alert legal if your required path crosses a rail line or other critical public access points. These are points at which striking workers could gather and disrupt transit in or out of the facility.

Consider the union's preparation for a strike. They are likely not making a plan specific to your upcoming bargaining, but instead have a generic approach mapped out that could be implemented with any of their negotiations. Look at the public-facing financial statements and related information filed by the union local.[7] You will be able to see what the local has set aside for their strike fund. This will be the fund they draw on if any of their bargaining units goes on strike and becomes eligible to receive support money from the union. Be sure to check the union's national information as well. For some unions, the local is not empowered to authorize a strike, only the national may do so.

---

[7] www.UnionFacts.com is a good place to start. Select Facts and Stats About the Labor Movement, then select the union and local. Be sure to click on the arrows to move to other screens for additional information. You should be able to locate an expense item called Strike Benefit, which is what employers loosely refer to as the "strike fund." The Office of Labor-Management Statistics (OLMS) publishes even more information than UnionFacts. The OLMS is the government entity responsible for enforcing the Labor-Management Reporting and Disclosure Act, which requires labor unions to file annual reports detailing their operations. The OLMS site is www.dol.gov/agencies/olms. Select Reports, Disclosures, and Decisions, then select Online Public Disclosure Room, then select Union Search. Sort and scroll to find the union and local to get to their LM-2, LM-3, or LM-4 form.

Weigh the information from these publicly facing financial filings against your policy on employees requesting PTO or advance pay, and consider when you would end medical and other benefits. All of this helps you understand the members' perspective. Will they be able to pay their own critical bills if they are not earning a paycheck?

Any work stoppage, even a short duration stoppage, does not just impact your employees and management team. Whether it's a legal strike, a wildcat strike, or a lockout by management, a work stoppage impacts the entire community in which you work as well as your organization's suppliers, vendors, and customers. They never forget its impact, ever. Expect that your organization's CEO will want to review and discuss your strike contingency plan once it's developed.

Budget and Executive Support

Both budgets should be pretty refined by now and should be shared with the appropriate executives. The CEO and perhaps other executives will need periodic updates on management's preparation.

Other Administrative Requirements

If you need to formally report your preparation to your in-house project management people, keep it high level. They are likely more interested in the use of personnel, so focus on that if you can rather than the detail of your white papers, for example. If you need IT to build confidential shared management sites, reach out to them early so they can build those sites discreetly. Identify who in IT you can call in if help is needed during negotiations.

Union's Preparation for Bargaining

Union representatives (employed by the union local with whom your organization has a CBA) negotiate labor agreements fairly frequently. Yours is not the only CBA they have and contract lengths vary, so they have probably more experience doing this that you do. I find that most union locals spend less time on the planning stage and focus instead on preparation.[8] For example, they review grievance topics for patterns. They solicit their members' input on topics via surveys, interviews, and/or meetings. Writing white papers in a structured fashion is not something you would anticipate a union doing, but you can expect them to have multiple optional proposals for a given topic in order to move incrementally from an extreme proposal to one that could be agreeable. Union leadership will have a solid understanding of how to cost out financial information. In response, management should be prepared to present supporting data to justify its proposals.

What do you imagine the union's critical "asks" will be at the table? Is there anything so big that management will not be able to find a way to respond to it with an acceptable counter? Is the union's biggest ask something they might be willing to strike over? Review your *risks and mitigation measures register*. Is there a concern on that list that is so big the union might strike?

Different unions invest different amounts of time and energy preparing for bargaining. Larger unions typically have in-house SMEs who can guide local union negotiators behind the scenes on wages and benefits. Sometimes to exert added pressure on management, the union SMEs might show up in the bargaining room, possibly introduced as observers for the union. Each side has the right to have whoever they want in the room so don't resist if this happens, although you can certainly ask why they are there. You can also respectfully challenge any assertions they make and request support data or analysis if you like.

Shortly before bargaining begins, the union leadership will typically survey the members of the bargaining unit to hear their current concerns and gather information that helps them prioritize the proposals they will be presenting at the table.

---

[8] A book written for union leadership to methodically prepare for CBA bargaining is: *Contract Bargaining Handbook for Local Union Leaders, Second Edition*, by M.B. Better, revised by K. May. Arlington, VA: Bloomberg BNA, 2017. Management's Three Musketeers group would be wise to have a working understanding of this material to round out their anticipation of what could happen during bargaining.

Prepare for the Unexpected

As you anticipate the transition to Phase Three, circle back to the management negotiations team for one more round of brainstorming. This time focus on what might happen during bargaining that hasn't yet been anticipated. What proposal might the union bring forward that got missed earlier? What possible union response might happen as a result of a management proposal? What might cause them to walk out of the room or worse? Without asking employees or supervisors directly, what is the current mood of the employee and supervisor populations? What is the current mood of your executive colleagues? Have there been any significant changes to the union leadership's relationship with the chief stewards, stewards, and/or members? Who are the key decision makers on the union side? These are all elements that you considered earlier in the planning and preparation phases, but time has moved on and it's possible that there has been an important change. And it's possible that that change is impactful enough to suggest that the assumptions that were part of the foundation of your earlier plan need to be revisited and possibly some of your proposals need to be refreshed or have their priorities reconsidered. Neither planning nor preparation should ever be static. They are never simply finished. This continuing evolution supports your agility during bargaining.

Top-Ranked Priorities

Before you head to the bargaining table, meet one more time with management's negotiating team to review the list of management's proposals. Identify your top three to five items and phrase them as interests or concerns, as opposed to specific language for the CBA. Be specific. I like using SMART goals—Specific, Measurable, Achievable, Realistic, and Timebound—however, framing bargaining goals as SMART goals is not always realistic. If your top goal is strengthening the union–management relationship, that doesn't mean that you agree to everything the union proposes. How would you measure success if the relationship is a goal? Might it be by the percentage of eligible members who vote to ratify the proposed CBA?

Agreement on the top priorities ensures that management's negotiations team members understand which proposals to fight hard for. It helps to manage the temptation to engage in lengthy debates on less important topics. And lastly, confirm that your CEO supports these priorities and while the CEO and perhaps others might like to be kept informed, it will limit any suggestion that you don't have the authority to bargain within the boundaries already agreed to. When bargaining is all said and done, your team and CEO will know what success looks like just by assessing your success on these few items that you identified in Phase One.

For one negotiation, our high priorities looked like like Table 2.3.

Table 2.3 Management's confidential high priorities, scenario one

✓	Retain management rights language
✓	Increase duration of short-term assignments from 120 to 180 days
✓	Revamp compensation structure; provide market competitive increases
✓	Term of CBA at four or more years

For a different negotiation, we had just one high priority item, as shown in Table 2.4.

Table 2.4 Management's confidential high priorities, scenario two

✓	Get random drug testing including processes into the CBA

Confirm Economic Budget

The original Three Musketeers should check in again with the CEO for a candid conversation focusing on management's top-ranked priorities and the economic budget to ensure understanding.

Keep Planning and Preparing

You will continue to plan and prepare as you enter and move through Phase Three and Phase Four. These are never-ending steps necessary to sustain your agility, your ability to identify and respond to opportunities and threats. It's important that you have an up-to-date tool kit, prepared for what will definitely happen next, what will probably happen next, and what could happen next.

Consider a professional improvisation troupe. They appear to react in real time, but in fact, they are practiced and well-rehearsed with multiple potential scenarios planned out. Improv is not unprepared. It is not reactive. It is prepared and agile.

All the work that you and your team have already done in Phase One and Phase Two pays off in Phase Three. Bargaining is the payoff for planning and preparation. During bargaining, you will continue to plan and prepare for the next session, the next day, the next CBA negotiation. Phase Three of this guide describes how you can continue planning and preparing by giving you tools to work with and the reasons why you should consider them.

PHASE THREE

Negotiate

Elements or preparation steps for the reader to select from in this chapter are listed in the recommended order of succession. You select the steps you wish to use based on your organization's needs and the context in which you will be bargaining.

My first failed negotiation happened when I was in high school. My mother, who was very old school, insisted that there were just three respectable professions for a young lady—teacher, nurse, and concert pianist. She was especially enthralled with the concert pianist idea because, in her mind, it allowed for a respectable reason to travel. And so, I began piano lessons in first grade, continued them weekly, supplemented them with practice seven days a week, one to two hours per day, every week, right into high school. I was good. I was the golden child.

Then I heard jazz for the very first time and immediately wanted to learn how to play it. Instinctively I knew my parents would not pay for or even allow formal lessons, so I tried for something more reasonable. In our household, one had to obtain permission in advance for anything our parents did not suggest, so I requested permission to teach myself jazz piano. I reported that I was not asking forgiveness for the many hours of weekly practice that I was already doing or forgiveness for chores and other learning opportunities already committed to. Jazz would be in addition to all of that. Their answer was an absolute no; no explanation was given; and no discussion was possible.

After multiple tries with the same basic request, I put my foot down firmly and informed my father that if they would not support this simple request, I would cease all classical piano playing immediately. No longer did they need to invest that money in my future. All the money they had spent on this since I was in first grade would go down the drain.

I went on strike without even knowing the idea. I was certain they would protect their investment and would allow me an hour or two of jazz each week. I was the golden child. And I was wrong. I didn't play any-thing on the piano again until decades later, long after I tired of reliving that debate.

I learned many lessons in my first failed negotiation: *do not* negotiate against yourself; *do* anticipate probable responses from the other party; and *do not* bluff unless you can live with the possible negative conse-quence of your bluff being called. I negotiated against myself; I didn't anticipate any outcome beyond the one I wanted; they called my bluff. My strike failed. It was an emotional negotiation on my part, completely lacking in planning and preparation. I wanted what I wanted. I got noth-ing but heartburn and heartache. And I learned: "Negotiation is work. It demands concentration, resilience, and creativity in a context where the stakes may be high and outcomes uncertain."[1]

Phase One is about planning. It is the 30,000-foot view of the terrain ahead. Phase Two is about detailed preparation. It is the topographic map with alternative routes carefully plotted. Phase Three is the actual real-time interaction of bargaining with the other party. It is the legally man-dated, rather regimented back-and-forth process of negotiating a new collective bargaining agreement. People often think of labor negotiations as a chess game or a poker game or a football game or even as a kind of warfare. Each of those ideas applies, but none covers the entirety of labor negotiations.

Some suggest that warfare might fit most closely. One side makes some moves, the other side reacts and responds, then the first party reacts and responds, and so on, back and forth. Progress is nonlinear; it does not move in a predictable or straight-line manner. It is more than the sum of its parts. It is adaptive, organic. Your side has plans and will adjust those plans in response to what it believes the union side is proposing. The union will often not come at you straight on, but instead from the side, or using an end run, if you will. Back and forth, then more back and forth. Time is required; it's part of the process. The ultimate outcome cannot be predicted.

This guide discusses process elements connected with bargaining so that you go into each bargaining session prepared and agile, but bear in

---

[1] M. Wheeler. 2013. *The Art of Negotiation: How to Improvise Agreement in a Chaotic World* (New York, NY: Simon & Schuster), p. 96.

mind, this guide doesn't describe *how to* bargain. Other books address that aspect. This *prepares* you to bargain. Remember the earlier calendar that showed negotiations as one of several activities? It was placed at the bottom of the calendar for a reason—it happens after much planning and preparation have already occurred.

Timing

Work with the union leadership to determine when the parties will offer each other the list of team members who will be at the table. Most likely, some or even all of the union's negotiations team members will be from your organization's employee population, so reach out to each team member's immediate supervisor to remind them of expectations—no conversations with that person (or any union employee) regarding any negotiation aspect—and ensure the supervisor has a plan to cover that person's normal work on negotiations days.

Preagreements

A number of things need to be discussed and agreed to by the parties before you start the formal process of bargaining. *Preagreements* is simply a term for agreements that must be reached before you can tackle the labor agreement itself. Typical preagreements needed before you can begin bargaining include:

- *Schedule for bargaining.* The usual rule of thumb is to begin bargaining one to three months prior to the current CBA's expiration date. Discuss with the union what the schedule for negotiations is expected to be. This will be an interesting signal as to how difficult the union anticipates negotiations to be. Because your union colleagues have so much experience at the table and have negotiated many other contracts, they will have a good sense of how many days will be needed. You will likely accept whatever their suggestion is for how many bargaining days and at what frequency. But what if the bargaining process goes longer or ends sooner, how will that be treated? This needs to be in place before you can move to the next step.

My experience includes a wide range of bargaining durations. The shortest was a few half-day sessions, totaling five or six full days altogether. One of the most intense used a long-established practice that was just two weeks. On a Wednesday the parties exchanged their entire list of proposals and each side walked the other through those proposals at a high level that day. The following Monday began one week of full day bargaining. In the second week, we were told we might bargain around the clock, 24 hours a day, every day that week, with the CBA set to expire Saturday at midnight. The last two or three days were always utterly exhausting.

My last bargaining experience anticipated 30 days of bargaining to occur in a four-month window, and we ended up canceling just a few of the calendared days. Noneconomic items were put to bed before the parties moved to economic items. For each set, the union provided their proposals first since they were the party wanting to change the current CBA.

- *Bargaining location.* You need to understand the expected schedule in order to determine the location for bargaining and negotiate the terms and cost with that facility. Work with the union to consider options, visit them together if agreeable, and then make a joint decision about location and how the cost will be shared, if it is shared.

- *Bargaining style and process.* There are two idealized styles of bargaining plus any number of hybrid or modified approaches. The most common for private sector bargaining is called *traditional* negotiations. It is also called *distributive bargaining* or *zero-sum game.* It's similar to poker in that neither party shows its hand, and bluffing might be a tactic at the table. Typically, each side presents a "great to have" proposal (without describing it that way) and already has in mind an "acceptable" version of that same proposal. They propose champagne, but will accept beer. You could also imagine a sports stadium; each side starts in the parking lot or bleachers of the stadium, then, through a series of back and forth moves, expects to find common ground somewhere on the playing field. With traditional bargaining, whenever the parties reach agreement on a language change to the CBA, there will be no clear understanding by either side if the agreed upon end point left something on the table or even resolved the inferred problem that the parties were working to address.

The other idealized method of bargaining is called *interest-based bargaining (IBB)*. The parties follow an agreed upon process to clearly identify a problem or concern that needs to be solved. Then they methodically and candidly discuss each side's interests or concerns associated with the problem, and identify interests or concerns that both parties share. Next, they follow a structured process to identify possible solutions, and ultimately rank the solutions. The highest ranked solution is normally what the parties adopt. IBB takes a lot of time. However, because the outcomes are developed jointly, the membership is thought to be more accepting of the changed CBA. More information about IBB is in Appendix A.

Documentation

Why should you reduce the parties' key agreements to paper signed by both parties? You do that so you have evidence to support your position in future debates. Debates might be as simple as an internal disagreement or misunderstanding about intent or practice, or they could be grievances over implementation of changed or new CBA language. Or, they could be legal challenges involving outside parties such as attorneys, mediators, arbitrators, or judges. Outside parties put great weight on documents created in real time and signed by the parties. They don't know the witnesses, after all, and any assessment of witness credibility has to be subjective.

Rules and Guidelines for Bargaining

While not legally mandated, it is very helpful for the parties to agree in advance to rules and guidelines about the process to be used in bargaining. This information is intended to supplement the legally required elements and will be distributed to negotiations team members on both sides, who constitute the audience for this document. They are typically less experienced with bargaining than their chief spokespersons and this document should help address their questions and set expectations.

Recommended elements to discuss with the union first and then document in your *rules and guidelines* document include: the dates and location planned for bargaining, the organizational structure of the combined bargaining team, names of each side's chief spokesperson(s), names of each party's negotiations team members who will be at the table, negotiation schedule and hours to be paid, roles and assignments, and definitions of terms such as *tentative agreement (TA)* and *final tentative agreement*. Consider including information about resources to be used and subject matter experts, comparator contracts (if any), joint and separate communication expectations as well as confidentiality expectations, information requests, note taking, language changes, implementation plan, rules of conduct, the sequencing of the different large segments of bargaining, and so on.

The union chief spokesperson and management chief spokesperson should both sign the document to demonstrate that both parties intend to follow these rules, something that may be important in managing the bargaining process in real time or in potential downstream legal debates around whether the agreed upon process was followed. Plan to review the document with the joint bargaining team on the first day of bargaining and answer any questions. A sample guideline is in Appendix B.

Note Taking

Notes are the record of the discussion of the proposals and how they changed during bargaining. They are a map of how the parties reached a *final tentative agreement*. Why do you need notes about bargaining discussions? The most frequent reason they will be used is when there is a contract dispute. They speak to the intent behind the language change. The notes will supplement or support or even correct individual memories when you are addressing grievances and concerns particularly in the first year or two of the new CBA.

Notes are also the record that demonstrates that you followed the National Labor Relations Board's (NLRB)'s requirements around give and take during bargaining, changing positions, and so on. The NLRB has the authority to confirm that the parties acted appropriately. Documents written in real time are the perfect evidence. Your notes are critical for any legal debate involving an outside party such as attorneys, mediators, arbitrators, or judges. It's all part of your big picture planning work—what will you need in the future if things do not go well? Planning and preparing for possible bad outcomes will help you achieve a better outcome in the long run.

Each party will take their own notes of the formal bargaining discussions. These are the only discussions that need to be documented. Notes taken by typical bargaining participants are what is expected. There is no need to use a court reporter or stenographer to capture verbatim notes; the financial burden would be an unusual expense for CBA bargaining.

I have never provided a copy of my team's notes to the other side. Instead, when needed, I report to them a brief summary or overview of what I read when I reviewed our notes, including if the desired detail is missing. That said, there may be times when you will need to provide your team's notes to an outside party.

When I was early in my labor career, every single person on management's negotiations team did their best to take verbatim notes in longhand for each session. Having laptops in the room was not yet a common practice. All those 8½ × 11-inch legal pads for each person were made part of management's formal record of bargaining. I remember two full file cabinet drawers of notes for each CBA negotiation. And while we occasionally went back through those messy handwritten notes, we were rarely able to really read them.

I approached our company's corporate chief negotiator with a request to use my laptop for the next CBA negotiations notes. We "demonstrated" to the union's chief negotiator that my hands had been injured from all my years of piano playing and that using a laptop seemed to be a reasonable accommodation. The union agreed to my unusual request. This was our corporation's first use of laptops for note taking. We could now search through bargaining notes for keywords and report with confidence our version of how the agreed-to language was achieved. And we could address the inaccurate reports from a problematic chief steward who historically asserted that he was present for a particular discussion, when in fact, according to the time stamps I added to my notes, he was out of the room on a personal smoke break.

More recently, I like a total of three management note takers to ensure complete coverage. Thanks to all my piano playing, I'm a fast and accurate typist so my notes are close to verbatim, but notes do not have to be verbatim. In addition to capturing the start and end times of each bargaining session and attendees present or absent, management's note takers should capture key elements for each topic: who is presenting (union or management, plus the name of the presenter), the CBA citation and brief descriptor, list any handouts or support documents provided, briefly summarize the discussion points made by each side, and clearly identify the status (new, accepted, modified, declined, or TA'ed for tentatively agreed to). Note takers should listen for and capture any discussion of intent, that is, why the language change is recommended. It amazes me how clear we think we are about the *why* at the table, only to be at odds about it once the contract is in place.

By using three management note takers, once the new CBA has been implemented, you will be able to report to the union that you reviewed the notes from all of management's note takers and found they all said "x" rather than what the union is asserting. The union will have one fairly good note taker, likely not multiple note takers, so there's a strong likelihood that management will win any debate that centers on reviewing bargaining notes.

I like to use a template to prepopulate a header for each bargaining session to show who is present. Sometimes people will be present for a morning session, but not for that day's afternoon session, for example. Some people will be gone for a week or two for vacation or illness. As the session gets underway, I count noses in the room and make a note of anyone who is missing. Here's a sample template to consider, as shown in Table 3.1.

Table 3.1 *Note taking template: prepopulated header*

7-10-20xx Wednesday		Start time xxxx a.m.	End time xxxx p.m.
Union	Name 1 Name 2 Name 3—absent Name 4	Name 5 Name 6 Name 7 Name 8	Chief Spokesperson Name Second Chair Name
Management	Name 1 Name 2 Name 3 Name 4	Name 5 Name 6—absent Name 7 Name 8	Chief Spokesperson Name Second Chair Name
Guests	None		
Location	Hotel Name, City, State		

After each day ends, I review my notes and insert a simple summary for that day, listing which topics were introduced, discussed, or TA'ed. Something like this, presented in Table 3.2, works nicely.

Table 3.2 *Note taking template: proposals passed across the table*

PROPOSALS PASSED ACROSS THE TABLE TODAY and TA'ed ITEMS (if any) mm-dd-yyyy
Company's counter on noneconomic items: • Article 9—not ready yet to present • Article 3—Seniority • Article 2—General Provisions Union's counter on noneconomic items: • Article 6—Employee Displacement • Article 7—Performance Development and Management • Article 8—Attendance • Article 14—Disability • Article 20—Grievance and Mediation • Article 3—Seniority • Article 2—General Provisions Items that were TA'ed today: • Article 3—Seniority

Daily Moves Summary

If you are a list maker like I am, you can use these summaries to efficiently build a spreadsheet that shows day by day which articles were introduced for discussion, offered counter-proposals, and reached a TA. That spreadsheet can reveal interesting trends which may inform adjustments to your current bargaining strategies and which will also inform your next CBA negotiation preparation. They can also be a quick reference point for refuting the union when, after the new CBA is in place, they want to discuss a certain topic one more time. You simply say that bargaining was just completed and this topic was discussed "x" number of days, so let's allow the new language to settle in for a while before we spend any more time on it. Go ahead, make my day.

Instead of waiting until bargaining is complete to build your spreadsheet summarizing the daily moves, assign one of the management team members to develop it in real time using an Excel spreadsheet. List the CBA articles down the left side, and plan for each column to represent a single bargaining session (as opposed to a single day that might have two or more distinct sessions). In the column header, note the date and start time of the specific session, as well as which party is presenting. As proposals are presented across the table, simply use a kind of shorthand in the appropriate cells indicating whether the proposal is an initial proposal (IP), counter-proposal (CP), or tentative agreement (TA).

And here's the magic about Excel spreadsheets: use the *comments* tool for each cell to briefly capture the reasons given for the suggested changes. Don't try to capture their verbatim explanation, but rather, focus on noting the keywords of the explanation. The comments remain hidden until the cursor hovers over the cell, however, you can opt to have them show, and there is an option of printing them out.

A sample "daily moves summary" is shown in Table 3.3.

The value of this high-level snapshot of the bargaining action is to flush out patterns such as how many times a noneconomic or economic topic was discussed, and to provide a quick summary of the stated reasons for a given proposal. This document complements the notes that others are taking which include lots of details (who attended, who presented, clarifying questions and responses). It is a valuable tool in your toolbox

Table 3.3 Daily moves summary

Article	Apr 6 9:00 a.m. Union	Apr 6 1:00 p.m. Mgmt	Apr 8 10:00 a.m. Union	Apr 9 9:00 a.m. Mgmt	Apr 10 9:00 a.m. Union	Apr 10 11:00 a.m. Mgmt
5—Performance	IP*	CP	CP	CP	CP	TA
6—Working Conditions	IP	CP	CP	CP	TA	
7—Displacement	IP			CP	CP	CP

*IP = Initial Proposal; CP = Counter-Proposal; TA = Tentative Agreement

and gives you the agility to anticipate, plan, and prepare for upcoming bargaining sessions.

Aspirational Remarks

Management's chief spokesperson should set the tone at the table by making some aspirational remarks that are welcoming and professional, and which set expectations. There are at least two instances in which this should be done. The first is at the very beginning of bargaining before any proposal is presented. If the parties have agreed to negotiate noneconomic proposals first, then the second set of remarks should be at the beginning of the economic bargaining, and should be made before any economic proposal is handed across the table. If the parties have not separated the topics into noneconomic and economic, then find some other small break in the talks in which the second set of remarks could fit.

Management's chief spokesperson is the leader not only of the management bargaining team, but also a recognized senior leader for the entire employee population. These are your employees sitting across the table from you. Make sure they respect you and value your opinion. Make sure they understand that you value their ideas and proposals, and that your consideration of their suggested changes is sincere and appreciated. In a very real sense, bargaining is a structured conversation about options for improving how we work. The course and outcome of a true conversation are not actually predictable, although the more agility you have built into your preparation for bargaining, the more opportunity you will have to influence the conversation in positive ways. Sample aspirational comments are in Appendix C.

The union also might or might not make some aspirational remarks. Invite them to go first so you can make any needed adjustments to your planned talking points. Even if the union opts to not offer any opening remarks, management should proceed. Again, you are the leader of everyone at the bargaining table other than the one or two people paid full time by the union. Your tone and remarks will influence the emotional response of the bargaining participants on both sides of the table. You are building trust and loyalty. You are calming the union's anxiety levels. This is your family; these are your people.

Roles of Management's Negotiating Team Members

The chief spokesperson and second will likely be doing most of the talking to offer management's proposals and counter-proposals. However, it's very common to ask another member of the team to speak on a given topic and take questions from the union. It shows that as a team you are united and frankly, it shares the load of presenting. When one of the designated note takers is asked to talk, just be sure that the other two are at hand so there are still at least two sets of notes for the future.

What do the other team members do during these sessions, what is their role? They should be actively listening and watching the body language of the union team members. Body language is another way of communicating. It's useful to know which union team members reacted in what manner to the union's proposal or to management's proposal. In management's private caucus session, the team should discuss what they observed so they know how much to push or whether to soften a proposal. In your caucus session, remind yourselves about your worst-case scenarios and strive to make adjustments to stay clear of them so you can focus on your best-case scenarios. Reflect on your own team members' body language and consider how the union may have perceived it. Thinking about body language helps the observer be aware of their own and fellow team members' unspoken signals.

Making Proposals and Counter-Proposals

This is where those white papers come in. You should have them at hand so you can review them in your caucus room. Remember, the white papers are only for management's use, not to be shared with the union. For any given topic that was anticipated, you should have data and some analysis to confirm, clarify, or refute the problem that is being raised. Look at the language that the management team drafted in Phase Two, as you can likely use that language either as is or with some small modification. Report your data or analysis at the table to support your proposal. Then hold your position until the union formally responds. The better your white paper on a given topic, the easier this becomes at the table. Remember that you don't have to change your position on every topic. Sometimes it's good to agree to disagree and it's okay to say so. Your earlier preparation gives you the agility to change or to choose to not change.

Economics

There are some approaches that not everyone knows, but they are permissible and can be very useful at managing the union's attention. One approach has to do with "bundling" proposals together to be considered as a package. Another approach is to preplan management's response to an economic proposal from the union and do so without causing more grief for the company. Let's explore both of these.

- *Bundling* is a way to present proposals that are closely connected or integrated. When you do this, you tell the union that you would like them to be discussed together. Let's say management wishes to present counter-proposals on language changes to five articles of the CBA. Management sees these articles as closely connected or integrated, and would like them to be discussed together. Tell the union that changes to one of these five will likely mean a change to one or more of the others of the five. Let them know that you do not wish to see any carve-outs from this group of five articles. Inform the union that you are looking for the union to either agree or counter as a bundle.

  When linking items as a bundle, include proposed CBA language that shows the connection of the articles as a bundle. Negotiations notes are a great resource if there's a downstream dispute, however, adding a sentence or two to the CBA that describes the link is even better and helps the union membership (your employees) understand the connection. It also serves as great evidence if a debate goes to an outside legal authority.

- *Responding to the union's economic proposals* can be challenging. If management's answer is too direct, too blunt, or suggests that the union's proposals are too expensive, it can leave the door open for the union to request to see the company's books. Allowing them to do so will likely slow down the bargaining process while they try to find opportunities to pursue their suggestions.

There are many ways to say "no" without directly saying "no." Before bargaining starts, prepare for these difficult conversations by assembling a confidential list of sample responses. You could have your management team members each select one or two to use so that the whole team doesn't use the same response. This should keep you from becoming frustrated and inadvertently opening the door for the union to see your books. Appendix D is a brief list of "no" responses to use as a starting point to write responses in your own voice. This preparation will pay off as you become more agile at the table.

Redline the CBA

All the proposals that have been tentatively agreed to during bargaining need to be captured in a single redlined CBA. Consider assigning this work to a detail-oriented team member and asking them to update the redlined document at some frequency such as weekly. That will save you a lot of time at the end of bargaining when you have multiple other competing priorities connected to implementation. A redlined CBA is critical for the union's information and ratification meetings as well as for management's subsequent training of supervisors, managers, and employees once the proposed contract is ratified.

Start with the CBA that is expiring and edit it showing all the agreed to language changes as redlined edits. Make sure the redlined edits align perfectly with the TA'ed documents from bargaining. When there is a disconnect, work with the union to resolve the discrepancy. You may need to involve the chief spokesperson from each side or refer to the negotiations notes to confirm understanding.

One union we negotiated with had the annoying habit of not sharing the same redlined documents at the table, so as a result, there was unneeded debate over the final language even when the intent was not an issue. During bargaining, it is critical to double check the counterproposals to ensure all the intended wording continues. That helps to prevent downstream debates including when building the full redlined CBA.

The union will probably use the redlined CBA in their information meetings with their members. You and your management team will also use the redlined CBA in your training of supervisors and managers about the changes that were agreed to.

Member Vote and Ratification

As the parties progress through bargaining, they reach small agreements along the way and label those as *tentative agreements* with the understanding that they might need to revisit one or more of those agreements due to a subsequent tentative agreement. Once all the topics have been TA'ed, the parties have reached a *final tentative agreement*. The union needs to present the proposed new CBA to their members and conduct a confidential vote to ratify the proposed agreement. This is normally done off the clock and off company property to demonstrate that management is not trying to influence their vote. No management person should attend these meetings or ask union employees about them.

There may be times when the union is concerned about member turnout, and so they might ask that these meetings be held on company time. If this happens and if you agree to their request, be sure to document the agreement and communicate it with the union employees and company supervisors. You might decide to pay each member one hour, for example, to attend a meeting of unknown duration. Ask the union to confirm attendance so you know who to pay. Importantly, insist that the union conduct the vote separately from the meetings and off company time. Document your full agreement with the union, again with both parties signing the agreement.

The union's chief spokesperson will inform management's chief spokesperson of voting results. In addition to the percent of yea's and nay's, it is useful to know how many people voted out of the total number of eligible voters. A low turnout for voting suggests a lack of emotional investment in the new CBA or a lack of faith in the union, either of which will likely concern you. If a low turnout happens, consider engaging your organizational effectiveness team in some team building to bring the union employees more in line with the company's strategic vision.

PHASE FOUR

Implement

Elements or preparation steps for the reader to select from in this chapter are listed in the recommended order of succession. You select the steps you wish to use based on your organization's needs and the context in which you will be bargaining.

Phase One was the high-level strategic planning, Phase Two was the topographic map that anticipated the details that the boots on the ground might need, and Phase Three was a bit about the actual negotiations or bargaining process. Phase Four is about management's implementation of the new CBA. In most cases, changes from the new CBA will be fully implemented within three months of ratification, often much sooner.

Phase Four is when you quickly develop and implement your communication and implementation plans, debrief executives and stakeholders, and set about updating processes and systems. All of this happens while you are simultaneously working on publishing the print and electronic editions of the new CBA. How quickly and how well you can do this depends largely on your advanced planning and preparation.

Timing

Start your Phase Four work while the union is holding its ratification meetings and voting, but be careful to not roll out anything until you have the formal voting results. Not every proposed CBA passes. Sometimes the parties have to return to the table for some additional bargaining and then repeat the informational meetings and voting process. Begin the Phase Four work before the CBA is ratified, but again, wait until the contract is approved by the membership before you proceed with your communication and implementation plans.

Communication and Implementation Plans

While the union is holding their information meetings and ratification vote, you should polish your plans around communicating and implementing the new CBA. Determine who needs to know what and when, and then decide what information each stakeholder or group will need. How will you get that information pulled together in a manageable form so you can report it clearly and concisely?

Calendar #4

This calendar is a detailed task list that includes firm implementation dates. Most likely, everything you will need to develop this calendar is in the new CBA. Review the full redlined CBA again, this time article by article looking for specific dates for new or changed processes, or when wage and benefits changes become effective. If no specific date is listed in the CBA, use the start date of the CBA. Identify an owner for each task or activity, most likely a manager or higher. Remember that not all items will change at the same time or even in the same calendar year, although some things might change immediately. Develop your draft calendar and review it as soon as possible with the activity owners to inform them, answer clarifying questions, and to make edits to your calendar. A basic format to consider for your calendar of CBA changes is shown in Table 4.1.

Supervisor Training

Using the redlined CBA and Calendar #4, start developing the training needed for supervisors of bargaining unit employees and their managers. Develop handouts or electronic resources including the redlined CBA for the supervisors to refer to both in the meeting and outside of the meeting. Identify management SMEs for them to reach out to later when they have questions on a given topic. For the training sessions, it's helpful to set up

Table 4.1 Calendar #4: Detailed task list with implementation dates

Article Section	Activity (Include communication step where appropriate)	Owner	Effective Year 1 20xx	Effective Year 2 20xx	Effective Year 3 20xx
1.3	Review number of contractor personnel in Q1 each year	Jim J.	Mar 31	Mar 31	Mar 31
5.1.6	Increase pay for on-call assignments starting 12-01-20xx, then annually thereafter (3.0% per year per 10.2.2)	Ron D.	n/a	Dec 01	Dec 01
5.1.6	On-call recognition pay: Issue on second regularly scheduled paycheck in January	Ron D.	Jan 10	Jan 10	Jan 10
10.3.1	Calculate and communicate the cost-of-living allowance (COLA) adjuster for 12 months ending in June. Include as part of communication for updated wage scale effective Dec 1 annually.	Leila R.	Nov 01	Nov 01	Nov 01
10.3.2	Publish and distribute updated wage scales in November each year for increases effective December 1, 20xx and annually thereafter (see 10.2.2.1 and 10.3.1)	Leila R.	Nov 01	Nov 01	Nov 01
15.2.1	A Covered Retiree becomes eligible for Retiree Medical	Robin	n/a	n/a	Jan 1
17.2.1	RKSP (401(K) Plan): Effective Year 3, change the matching contribution to equal 50% of the RKSP Participant's elective deferral	Robin	n/a	n/a	Jan 1

a template, one topic per page, so attendees can easily follow along. An example that works nicely as a PowerPoint slide is shown in Table 4.2.

Table 4.2 Template for training supervisors

Topic	Paid Time Off (PTO)
What changed	• 8 hours of PTO added to annual accrual, effective June 1st • No minimum usage requirement for employees with less than one year of service • Buy-back provision cannot reduce PTO balance below 32 hours (okay to use PTO below 32 hours, but may not buy back below 32) • Requests for buy-back must be submitted before December 1st
Why	• To offset the increased wait period for STD benefits • Encourage new employees to build up their PTO bank
Supervisors' actions	• Develop or refresh your work group's scheduling guidelines to ensure consistency with the PTO language • By September 30, review (and refresh if needed) and communicate work group's guidelines for following year's PTO auction
CBA citation	Article 11 (Paid Time Off)
SMEs	Labor Relations Team, Benefits Team

Brief the Executives

Most likely you will invite your executive colleagues to the supervisor training, however, you may also find it useful to separately debrief them to allow more confidential discussion of some elements. For example, you may want to develop and confidentially share a scorecard with just the executives, using checkmarks or the green, yellow, and red shading associated with a simple scorecard, as shown in Table 4.3.

For your meeting with the executives, create a second confidential scorecard for what you believe the union's priorities were (without asking the union, of course). Unlike poker or other card games where the cards are revealed at the end, you may never learn the union's real priorities. Your assumptions are what you can report to the executives, as shown in Table 4.4.

Take time to assess the new state of the labor–management relationship. Is it better than before or worse? What needs to happen in the next few months to ensure the parties are moving forward as you had hoped?

Table 4.3 Confidential executive scorecard: management's priorities

Management's Confidential Priorities And Scorecard	High Priority	Medium Priority
• Retain management rights language	✓	
• Increase duration of short-term assignments from 120 to 180 days	✓	
• Re-vamp compensation structure; provide market competitive increases	✓	
• Term of CBA at four or more years	✓	
• Redefine attendance occurrence to be one day instead of one multiday event		✓
• Cap PTO usage at 30 days immediately prior to retirement or resignation		✓
• Retain or reduce health care and retirement costs to company		✓

Table 4.4 Confidential executive scorecard: union's assumed priorities

Assumed Union Confidential Priorities And Scorecard	High Priority	Medium Priority
• Reorganize collective bargaining agreement	✓	
• Re-vamp compensation structure; ensure market competitive wage increases	✓	
• Retain or reduce health care and retirement contribution cost to employee	✓	

Be sure to review your notes from the earlier briefings you did with the CEO and your executive colleagues. How did you define success then? Hopefully your anticipated indicators of success align with the final scorecard. The ideal world would have management, the union, and the union members all assessing the bargaining to be successful, even if each constituent is focusing on different measures. If there's a gap in the alignment, assemble your Three Musketeers team from Phase One, and discuss how to close that gap.

Employee Training

While you want to assume that the union informed all its members during its information meetings for ratification, management needs to also make time to train union employees on key changes in the new CBA. The focus will probably be on operational process changes, changes around job movement, and changes to benefits. Ask one of your management team members to review the redlined CBA article by article from the perspective of a union employee who did not attend a ratification meeting. Consider having supervisors deliver the training with one or more management negotiations team members in the room to help answer clarifying questions. Keep the training conversation focused on the language change, not the conversation or debate that resulted in the change.

Check in on the Implementation Process

Calendar time to check in either individually or as a group with managers who own the process and system changes. Make sure they are on track. Work with them individually to remove roadblocks. It is incredibly important to make sure that each element is rolled out according to the timelines in the new CBA and it's just as important to publish the new CBA as soon as possible. Failing to do so will negatively impact the morale of the union employees as well as their supervisors and managers, and could result in grievances for violating the new contract provisions.

Celebrate

Bring the joint negotiations team back together, both management and union, for a joint lunch or other celebratory event. It's great if the CEO and your executive colleagues join in. Thank the combined team for a job well done and acknowledge what a heavy lift it was for everyone. This helps to point the next chapter of labor–management relations in the right direction. Always think ahead—the planning and preparation for next time should never stop.

Lessons Learned (Part Two)

Ask management's negotiations team to offer their thoughts on lessons learned—what could have gone better, what was asked of them that wasn't needed, what could be more efficient next time, what worked well, that sort of thing. Capture these notes for planning and preparing for your next round of bargaining. Consider checking in with these same team members a year or so downstream to ask the same type of questions, this time with the added benefit of some experience with the new contract. You will refer back to these notes as you begin planning for the next CBA negotiation.

Final Thoughts

Late one Tuesday afternoon, after the union's members had ratified our proposed CBA, I received a phone call from a vice president of the regional office for that union. His signature was required on the new CBA. When he introduced himself, I guessed he was calling to offer his congratulations on the new contract and tell me that the fully signed agreement was on its way back to me. I immediately thought, what a nice gesture.

Instead, he wanted to threaten me. "You're new," he said, "you don't understand that there was an error made in the new language for the wage calculator. By writing it this way, it means that future pay increases will be based on a straight dollar amount instead of being based on percentages, which is how it has always been. That will reduce the amount of future earnings of our members in this pay classification. You're new and you just didn't understand the impact this has." I opened my copy of the red-lined contract and read the language out loud. "No, I responded, that's what was negotiated. We discussed the future impact this would have and the union people at the table agreed." "It's a mistake," he insisted, "you have to change it." "Just a second," I said, "I'm checking my notes from the bargaining session; yes, this is the language we all agreed to." "Listen to me," he continued,

> you have to go back to the prior language. Let me make sure you understand. I can't sign this contract. I'm giving you twenty-four hours to agree to the prior language, or we will put every plant in this industry in the state on strike. Is that clear? Twenty-four hours.

"I understand your words and that this is very serious. Since I'm new as you said, I'll reach out to the president of my company and I'll call you back after I talk with him. He's not here at the moment, so that may take some time." "Twenty-four hours," he growled as he hung up.

I walked down the hall and described the conversation to "Boss Jim." "Really?" he asked incredulously as he walked over to a bookcase and reached for a yellowed binder labeled *Strike Plan.* "There hasn't been a strike in this industry in, well, decades. Let me make some phone calls."

On Wednesday afternoon, some twenty-three hours and a few minutes after our first conversation, I returned the call to the vice president of the union. "We appreciate your concern," I explained, "but having double-checked our bargaining notes, we find this language accurately captures what was agreed to by the parties at the table. And the membership has already voted their approval of the proposed contract. I don't know how we would change the language at this point in time, especially given that we don't agree with the idea of changing the language." The vice president's voice was tense. "Listen," he said, "don't be stupid. You need to think this through. We will put every plant in the state on strike if you don't correct this error. Every plant. We have that power. I'm going to give you another twenty-four hours to rethink your position. You are stupid if you don't change." "I hear what you are saying, sir, and I will reach out to my president. Again, he is not here so it may take some time." "Twenty-four hours," he insisted as he hung up the phone.

Early Thursday morning, I received a phone call from the union business agent who was at the table. He was a seasoned rep who had worked this contract for many, many years. He said that he understood the regional office was upset and wanted to let me know that he would continue to support what was agreed to at the table and what the members had ratified. "Besides," he said, "they've threatened me before. I keep a cabin in the mountains that no one knows about and I've had my family up there since the contract was voted in. I was planning to retire this year anyway." I immediately reported this conversation to Boss Jim, who reached out to the business agent. "This is not worth putting your family or anyone in harm's way," Boss Jim explained to the rep, "we can live with the old language." "No sir," responded the rep, "we negotiated this in good faith. We knew what we were doing. And because of the most favored nation clause, I knew the impact would be bigger than just this facility. My family is safe and I've been carrying my gun for a few weeks now. I'm good."

That afternoon, twenty-three hours and a few minutes after last talking with the vice president of the union, I called again with our declination of his demand. He was more than angry and said something disrespectful about me being a female.

Here's my takeaway. Even if you are new or stupid or even female, if you negotiated in good faith, have good records of the discussion, and the membership ratified the agreement, there are times when one of the stakeholders—this time, a high-level official for the union's regional office—may be unhappy with the outcome. The threats he made were very real. This was a union known for aggressive stands and for lengthy, impactful strikes. The local rep made sure his family was safe and carried his own protection because the regional office had earned a nasty reputation over the many years that he had worked with them. While the threats were unsettling, the process requirements had been followed and the membership had supported the change. All that said, you and your organization are still in a relationship with this union—its members, the local business agent, and the regional and national offices. One big family, if you will, and no opportunity for you to divorce them.

Our management team had planned thoughtfully for bargaining the renewal of this CBA. It was a mature contract and the most favored nation clause added a level of stability that I've rarely seen in other contracts. Simply put, the wage structure had been in place for many years, was used in exactly the same way by all the parties recognized in the most favored nation, and was expected to remain unchanged for the rest of time.

And yet as we were preparing for bargaining, we challenged ourselves with an aspirational goal: reduce the wage burden for future years by modifying the wage structure itself. As I recall the prior structure, there was a single job classification that was used as a benchmark job. That was the one pay rate that was negotiated locally. All other pay rates were a certain percentage above or below the benchmark job, per the CBA. Our initial proposal was to change all pay rates to be a flat dollar rate higher or lower than the benchmark job, and after some back-and-forth proposals and much discussion, we landed on changing the pay basis of just the top-tier job to a flat dollar amount over the next highest paid job. This didn't mean much difference in actual pay rates for the first few years, but starting in about five years, the savings would be noteworthy.

At our facility, only one employee was impacted by this structural change, and after the contract was approved, he shared that he appreciated his pay rate being set closer to his co-workers' pay rates because it would mean they would be more accepting of him as an equal to them. His job was that of a working supervisor. He did the same tasks as his co-workers and in addition, each day he did some administrative work that the co-workers did not view as worthy of much additional pay. The co-workers readily supported the proposed structural change because it didn't impact them individually; it only impacted the one individual.

Although only the one individual was impacted at our facility, the impact extended to all the other parties connected through the most favored nation clause in our CBAs. We negotiated locally and achieved a widespread cost improvement over time for all these employers. We planned creatively for our negotiations, brainstormed a variety of approaches and responses, and navigated the bargaining to a place where a direct conversation could happen. If we hadn't planned and prepared so thoroughly and set such a lofty long-term goal, we wouldn't have had the agility to seize the opportunity when it presented itself.

Akai Ito

Akai ito is the Japanese term for the "red thread" of destiny. It refers to the life-long connection or red thread between two people or two entities. It can describe the link between two warriors repeatedly locked in battle over a lifetime, or to describe two lovers who meet, come together, become separated, and get back together. It can describe teacher and pupil encountering each other in a life-long relationship.

I use *akai ito* to describe labor-management relations. Sometimes the red thread is relaxed and smooth, other times it becomes twisted and snarled. Through it all, labor and management remain connected. You cannot separate them really, but you can work to infuse positive energy into the relationship and minimize emotional responses. Many people see themselves as victims and they want a union to speak for them not only during bargaining in particular, but in other times as well. Being an active listener and thoughtful communicator is key to a relaxed and smooth *akai ito*. Conversations are a form of partnership, after all.

When I began working in labor relations, real and feigned emotional outbursts were fairly common. Either party might literally storm out of a meeting in protest of the absurdity of the other side's comments. I was skilled at not reacting emotionally and instead remaining calm and professional. Over my 20+ years of negotiating on behalf of different companies, with different unions in different states, the drama and angst seem to have lessened. With each contract that I've helped negotiate, my increasing attention to and use of deep planning and preparation was the major reason for an improved *akai ito*. The red thread is less crimped.

Planning and preparing thoroughly for labor agreement negotiations is a proven way to keep those emotional outbursts at bay and importantly, to get the best possible outcome by anticipating the many variables that influence the process and the work of bargaining, leading to agility when facing difficult moments or unexpected opportunities. Similar to basic project management, it includes planning and preparing for personnel changes and considers unspoken individual agendas.

You probably won't use every recommendation in this guide for every CBA negotiation; however, if you refer to this guide as you plan and prepare, and select the most critical elements and timing for a given round, you can be confident that you are working toward the best possible result for your organization, and most likely, the union and its members (your employees) will also see their outcomes in a positive light. A smooth and well-tended *akai ito*.

APPENDIX A

Glossary

Below are brief explanations of how bargaining and negotiation terms have been applied in the context of this book.

Bargaining. This is the formal process of negotiations between the employer and the union. It usually refers to the process of negotiating a new collective bargaining agreement; however, it can also refer to the process of negotiating other formal agreements between the parties.

Benchmark job. This is a union job (also called a job classification) that is used as a reference point with other organizations for purposes of comparing compensation. It assumes that the essential job functions and any prerequisites are the same in the comparator organizations. Discussed in *Final Thoughts*.

Bundling is a way to present proposals that are closely connected or integrated. Discussed in *Phase Three: Negotiate.*

Caucus. A meeting of the negotiating team of one of the parties involved in negotiations. There are separate caucuses for management and union. A negotiations team member might request a caucus or a chief spokesperson might say that, "it's time to caucus," meaning a desire to talk separately with their own team members.

CBA. See *collective bargaining agreement.*

Chief negotiator (or chief spokesperson). This is each party's primary spokesperson at negotiations. They speak on behalf of their respective teams. They are empowered to make and accept proposals, and are authorized to make other agreements regarding the process.

Collective bargaining agreement (CBA). The labor agreement between the employer (aka, the company or the organization) and the union. It covers a specific period of time, typically between two and five years. Also called a *contract* or *labor agreement*.

Comparator CBAs. These are typically used for comparison of compensation, benefits, and sometimes, operating practices. To identify which organizations might be used for comparison, ask which unionized organizations does your company get its union employees from or lose them to? Not a required part of the process, but useful for understanding the market. Discussed in *Phase Two: Prepare.*

Contract. See *Collective bargaining agreement.*

Cost of living adjustment (COLA). Annual wage increases often include a COLA consideration, which itself is based in part or even entirely on changes to the consumer price index (CPI).

Daily moves. This is a management-only document that is created during bargaining or immediately afterward. It summarizes the proposals, counter-proposals, and support reasons for each, and is used to identify patterns for preparing for future bargaining. Discussed in *Phase Three: Negotiate.*

Dependencies. Refers to planning or preparation work that will have to be done before other work can be done, so it is said that one thing is dependent on another. In some instances, the dependency is driven by timing; other times certain work must be completed and is needed in order to do other work.

Distributive bargaining. See *Traditional bargaining.*

Economic proposals. CBA articles can typically be sorted by economic and noneconomic articles. Bargaining proposals involving economic articles are those *with* direct financial burden or financial connection such as employment guarantees, wages, health care, retirement plans, contract term, working conditions, paid time off, holidays, and other company-provided benefits. Contrast this with *noneconomic proposals.*

Federal Mediation and Conciliation Service (FMCS). The federal agency that engages with labor and management in the labor agreement bargaining process to ensure compliance with federal regulations. Provides process training as requested by the parties as well as mediation and mediation resolution services should bargaining stall. Discussed in *Appendix F: Resources.*

Final tentative agreement. The agreement reached by the employer and the union regarding all the proposed changes to the new CBA. The final tentative agreement is then presented by the union to the union members for ratification. Discussed in *Phase Three: Negotiate.*

First-time contract (or initial contract). This is the very first labor agreement between the parties. There are special NLRB rules around negotiating a first-time contract.

Grievance. A formal complaint filed by the union against the company. This typically challenges a discipline or asserts a violation of the CBA or past practice. Unresolved grievances may go to mediation and/or arbitration. Discussed in *Phase Two: Prepare.*

Hybrid bargaining process. This blends the two idealized bargaining processes of traditional bargaining and interest-based bargaining (IBB). Often a hybrid process will use IBB for noneconomic items and traditional for economic items. The parties should agree to the specific process to be used prior to the start of bargaining. Discussed in *Phase One: Plan* and in *Appendix B: Interest-Based Bargaining.*

Initial contract. See *First-time contract.*

Interest-based bargaining (IBB). This is a collaborative bargaining process in which the parties approach each other with concerns or problems to be jointly solved using candid, direct conversation. Discussed in *Phase One: Plan* and in *Appendix B: Interest-Based Bargaining.*

Labor agreement. See *Collective bargaining agreement.*

Legacy costs. Expenses to be paid today and in the future that are connected to past commitments particularly in the area of retiree benefits such as pensions, health care, and insurance. These are particularly burdensome for a company with a shrinking work force.

Lockout. See *Strike contingency plan.*

Management rights language. Language that specifically affirms that management (also called the company or organization or the employer) is responsible for running its operations. It confirms or establishes those rights, sometimes including a list of specific activities or decisions that are recognized by the union.

Memorandum of agreement (MOA). A formal agreement between the parties typically impacting the full membership. Some MOAs are expected to be incorporated into the next CBA. Also called MOA or MOU (memorandum of understanding). Discussed in *Phase Two: Prepare.*

Most favored nation (MFN) clause. A CBA provision that connects multiple employers and union locals in a named industry and/or region. If lower cost wages or benefits are agreed to in one CBA in the industry or region, a subsequent employer recognized in the MFN clause may demand that its CBA be modified to adopt the more favorable wages or benefit. See discussion in *Introduction* and in *Final Thoughts.*

Multiemployer CBA. One agreement covering multiple small independent companies in the same industry and multiple union locals from the same national union.

National Labor Relations Board (NLRB). The federal agency tasked with enforcing federal labor laws around collective bargaining and unfair labor practices. Cited in *Appendix F: Resources.*

Negotiations. The formal process of bargaining between the employer and the union. It usually refers to the process of bargaining a new collective bargaining agreement; however, it can refer to the process of bargaining other formal agreements (such as MOAs or MOUs) between the parties.

Noneconomic proposals. CBA articles can typically be sorted by economic and noneconomic articles. Bargaining proposals involving noneconomic articles are those *without* direct financial burden or financial connection such as seniority, job selection and assignment, employee displacement, performance, attendance, discipline, grievance process, and disability. Contrast this with *economic proposals*.

Notes. Refers to the bargaining notes taken by each party during formal bargaining sessions. These are the formal record of the discussion of proposals and how they changed during bargaining. Discussed in *Phase 3: Negotiate.*

Notice of bargaining (Form F-7). This is a simple form that informs the other side that it wishes to discuss a change to the current CBA. It also notifies the FMCS that their mediation help might be needed if negotiations stall. Discussed in *Phase One: Plan.*

Office of Labor-Management Statistics. Part of the federal government's Department of Labor (DOL). Discussed in *Phase Two: Prepare* and cited in *Appendix F: Resources.*

Parties. This refers to the employer (also called the company or the organization or management) and the union. The parties negotiate the CBA.

Picket line. One of the tools available to union members should a legal strike occur. A picket line is made up of striking workers who walk back and forth on public property and carry signs identifying their position in order to gain community support for their position. Discussed in *Phase Two: Prepare.*

Pie. An informal term referring to the full cumulative cost of every change through the life of the contract. Discussed in *Appendix D: Management's Chief Spokesperson's Opening Remarks—Sample.*

Preagreement is an informal term referring to an agreement that must be reached before you can tackle the labor agreement itself. Discussed in *Phase Three: Negotiate.*

Proposal. In the normal course of bargaining a labor agreement, one party begins the discussion by presenting its *initial proposal* of items (or CBA language) to be changed. The other party responds by *accepting* the proposal, making a *counter-proposal,* or stating they wish to stay with the *status quo.* Once agreement is reached on a particular item, it is said that the parties have a *tentative agreement* on that item. Each party has the opportunity to present *initial proposals.* See discussion in *Phase Three: Negotiate* and in *Appendix B: Bargaining Rules and Guidelines—Sample).*

Ratification. The formal vote by the union membership on whether to approve the proposed new labor agreement.

Redline. A standard function in Word and other word processing programs that allows one to show deleted language as being struck through (yet still readable) and newly added language with an underscore. Language that is moved to a different place within the document is shown with colored text and a double underscore.

Reopener. A clause within the CBA that is narrowly focused on a specific economic aspect of the CBA. A wage reopener is often based on changes to the Consumer Price Index (CPI) exceeding an identified threshold in a set time period prior to the end of the contract term. When triggered, this is the only topic to be bargained; all other CBA provisions must wait until the next regular CBA bargaining occurs.

Second chair. This is each party's second spokesperson at negotiations. In addition to being a recognized backup to their party's chief spokesperson, the second chair typically speaks on behalf of their respective teams and may share responsibility with the chief spokesperson for making and accepting proposals, and making other agreements regarding the process.

SHRM competency model. This model identifies specific competencies that could be used to determine individual training needs. See discussion in *Introduction*.

SMART goals. This is a common structure for defining business goals by ensuring each goal is Specific, Measurable, Achievable, Realistic, and Timebound.

Strike. See *Strike contingency plan*.

Strike contingency plan. This is management's confidential plan detailing how to run each aspect of its business if no union employees are available to work due to a strike or lockout. See discussion in *Phase One: Plan* and *Phase Two: Prepare*.

Strike fund (or strike benefit). This is the money the union local has set aside to pay union employees should a legal strike occur. Each union sets its own rules regarding how much money each striking employee will receive and when the money is to be issued. Discussed in *Appendix F: Resources*.

Subject matter expert (SME). Someone with recognized expertise in a particular subject or area. Compensation specialists are considered SMEs in compensation, for example. A long-tenured employee in a specific operational area might be considered an SME. Discussed in *Appendix C: Bargaining Rules and Guidelines—Sample*.

SWOT analysis. A structured way to consider a group's Strengths, Weaknesses, Opportunities, and Threats. Discussed in *Phase One: Plan*.

Tentative agreement (TA). When bargaining a new collective bargaining agreement, the parties will reach agreement on small parts of the agreement, often grouped by topics or by CBA articles. These smaller agreements are deemed *tentative agreements* as it is possible they might change in the course of discussing a subsequent provision. Once all the topics or articles of the CBA have been tentatively agreed to, the parties will designate the full CBA as a *final tentative agreement.* The union presents the final tentative agreement to the union membership for a formal vote (called *ratification*). Ratification is required to make the proposed new CBA official. Discussed in *Phase Three: Negotiate.*

Term of CBA. This is the effective period for a CBA, typically two to five years in duration. The effective start and end dates of the contract are given.

Total compensation statement. Individualized employee statements reporting both direct compensation such as base pay and incentive pay, and also indirect compensation such as the employer portion of health, dental, and vision plans, flexible spending accounts, and more. Discussed in *Phase Two: Prepare.*

Traditional bargaining. Also called *distributive bargaining* or *zero-sum game.* Discussed in *Phase Three: Negotiate* and in *Appendix B: Interest-Based Bargaining.*

Union representative *(or union rep or business agent).* An employee of the union who is paid to represent union members at one or more employers.

Union stewards and chief stewards. Company employees who are on-site union representatives by virtue of being voted into those roles by their union co-workers at the same company. Stewards and chief stewards typically continue to perform their bid jobs, are paid by the company, and are given time away from their bid jobs to investigate concerns and represent their union colleagues in discussions with management.

UnionFacts.com. Management-friendly website reporting a broad range of information about individual unions. Discussed in *Phase Two: Prepare.*

Union structure. Most unions have a tiered structure that includes a national office, a regional office and a local office.

U.S. Bureau of Labor Statistics (BLS). A federal agency tasked with tracking a wide variety of data about labor including work stoppages. Discussed in *Phase Two: Prepare*.

Wish list. An informal term for management's confidential list of possible proposals for bargaining. Discussed in *Phase Two: Plan* and *Phase Three: Negotiate*.

White paper. White papers are management's confidential, structured position papers, one per topic, that each identify a concern or problem, the current CBA language that is connected with the problem, the history of the language, and management's ideal and acceptable CBA language change(s) that would be needed to resolve the problem. Discussed in *Phase Two: Prepare*.

Wildcat strike. See *Strike contingency plan*.

Work stoppage. See *Strike contingency plan*.

Zero-sum game. See *Traditional bargaining*.

APPENDIX B

Interest-Based Bargaining

Interest-based bargaining (IBB) is used more frequently in public sector bargaining than in private sector. That said, IBB seems to be gaining popularity in the private sector in recent years, and some parties are moving to a hybrid blend of traditional and IBB. It is appropriate to share a bit of information about IBB so you have a sense of how it could work for your organization. Let's compare and contrast for some understanding.

Traditional distributive bargaining is often likened to playing poker where during the course of playing, the parties might bluff or even misrepresent their hands during the game, and they most definitely do not disclose which cards they are holding. However, at the end of the game, all the cards may be revealed and you have a sense of what the other player was working with. If you play cards with the same players in the future, you can gain some insight into their strategies by making mental notes during play and then seeing their cards at the end of a game.

But not with labor agreement negotiations. Most often, one of the outcomes of traditional CBA bargaining is that the parties never reveal, or allow to be disclosed, their primary goals or objectives. The back-and-forth process of changing positions, of proposals and counter-proposals, is so important that the parties rarely offer insight into what their top priorities are. A successful negotiation might be defined as surviving the process, and is rarely defined as achieving measurable goals or improving the labor–management relationship.

Emotionally it feels like you just bought a car. Congratulations, you just purchased a new sports car for an exorbitant price! Did you get all the bells and whistles you wanted? Did you pay more than what you planned to pay? Was that the best price possible? You'll never know, so you walk away unsettled, and hating car sellers because you have no confidence that the process worked for both parties.

When my brother and I were newly out of college, my brother decided he had saved up enough money to buy a new car and so he wanted to get rid of his old, very used car. The most common way to buy or sell a used car in those days was to use the local newspaper's Sunday classified advertising section. My brother preferred a more efficient method, which was to phone me to see if I wanted to buy the car. If he guessed correctly, it would save him the bother of placing the ad and answering lots of phone calls. I was agreeable, but neither of us knew how to set a price that would be fair to both of us. We decided to ask our dad to set a price since we believed Dad loved us pretty much equally.

The car was quite old and my brother had put no money into fixing it up or maintaining it save the occasional oil change and such. Dad suggested $300 was all that it was worth. That was acceptable to both of us so we pursued the deal. One year later, the car was crying out for expensive repair work so I put a *for sale* ad in my town's Sunday newspaper asking for $600 or best offer. A few phone calls and test drives later, the car sold for $600, not even a whisper of negotiating. I was ecstatic as I envisioned putting the $600 toward the down payment on a new car for myself. Imagine my surprise when I learned that both my dad and my brother thought I should split the newly found $300 with my brother. I pushed back: my brother lived in a big city and his newspaper reached many more people than the newspaper in my much smaller town. I was willing to talk with people and he wasn't. We had agreed on a price set by a neutral party and now a year later, they wanted to renegotiate because I had worked harder than my brother.

I often thought that first sale from my brother to me was like interest-based bargaining in that we agreed on a nontraditional process, used a neutral party for the hard part, and together agreed on the outcome. In comparison, the second sale that was by me to a stranger, felt more like traditional bargaining. I asked the stranger for a higher price than I expected to get and when I got it, I didn't suggest to the stranger or to anyone else that it was too much. I simply patted myself on the back for having the courage to ask for more.

Interest-based bargaining starts with a foundation of trust between the parties. Through structured conversations, the parties openly and candidly identify their top interests and concerns about a topic that they have agreed to discuss. Together they develop a concise problem statement, which is then worked on by a subteam comprised of members of both negotiating teams. That subteam's analysis and recommendations are brought back to the full negotiations team for review and approval. Documentation around intent and alternative solutions is developed jointly. Because solutions have been developed together, the overall bargained CBA is expected to be both more understandable to and better accepted by the membership, with fewer challenges to the changes being implemented with the new CBA.

While some private sector companies and their union counterparts are moving toward IBB, probably more are moving toward a hybrid or blended approach. With a hybrid approach, most likely they are using IBB for the noneconomic articles of the CBA, and then using traditional bargaining for the economic articles.

For any IBB, it is critical that the parties receive joint training along with opportunities to practice their new IBB skills, adding a bit of work and time to your Phase Two preparation. The Federal Mediation and Conciliation Service (FMCS) offers training on IBB[1]; however, it appears that the content and quality, and therefore the effectiveness and success, of that training varies significantly from one region to another. Explore options to offer training from different sources. Trainers experienced with labor–management relationships[2] or organizational effectiveness should be a consideration.

---

[1] The Federal Mediation and Conciliation Service offers training on alternative bargaining processes such as IBB. More information at www.fmcs.gov, then select Services, then select either Alternative Bargaining Processes or Labor Management Partnership Building.

[2] Restructuring Associates, Inc. is an excellent firm that provides support on labor–management relationships including training for interest-based bargaining. More information at www.restructassoc.com.

APPENDIX C

Bargaining Rules and Guidelines—Sample

Following is a hypothetical agreement about the rules and guidelines for bargaining that the chief spokespersons would have negotiated. The idea is to review it with the negotiations participants in the opening joint session before any proposal is handed across the table. The intent is to ensure that all participants, not just the chief spokespersons, are on the same page regarding process and behavior expectations. This gives you documentation to remind your counterpart of the expectations that the parties agreed to in advance. And it is evidence for any outside party (attorney, mediator, arbitrator, or judge, for example) of the parties' intent going into bargaining.

Sample Bargaining Rules and Guidelines

1. **Introduction.** This document outlines the process for negotiating the [20xx] collective bargaining agreement by and between UNION NAME ("the union") and COMPANY NAME ("the company," also referred to as "management"). Once this process guideline is finalized and agreed to in writing, any subsequent changes must be approved in writing by UNION CHIEF SPOKESPERSON and COMPANY CHIEF PERSON, or their designee.

2. **Dates planned for negotiation.** The parties have identified several dates between and including July 10, 20xx and October 31, 20xx as dates planned for bargaining. The parties hope that they will have a final agreement supported by the full negotiations team not later than MMDDYYYY. The preplanned bargaining dates are:
   - July 10, July 11, July 17, July 18, July 30, July 31.
   - August 1, August 6, August 7, August 8, August 26, August 27, August 28, August 29.

- September 3, September 4, September 5, September 16, September 17, September 19, September 30.
- October 1, October 3, October 14, October 15, October 17, October 28, October 29, October 30, and October 31.

3. **Location for bargaining and meals.** The parties have agreed to hold their planned negotiations at the [XXX Hotel] in CITY, STATE. Meeting rooms and food will be in the hotel's executive conference center and will be paid for by [COMPANY] and according to the agreement reached between the parties in MMYYYY. The parties have reserved one large meeting room (large enough to accommodate all the planned negotiations participants) plus two caucus rooms (one for management's participants and one for the union's participants). There will be no cost for parking on hotel property. Lunch and snacks at breaks will be provided to participants during each bargaining day.

4. **Notice of intent to bargain.** The union provided its formal notice of intent to bargain via [letter] dated MMDDYYYY from UNION CHIEF SPOKESPERSON to COMPANY CHIEF SPOKESPERSON.

5. **Roles and quorum.** The chief spokesperson for the union will be UNION PERSON. The chief spokesperson for the company will be COMPANY PERSON. COMPANY PERSON #2 will be the alternate chief spokesperson for the company in the event that COMPANY PERSON is not available.

- The union's negotiations team members will be [LIST NAMES].
- Management's negotiations team members will be [LIST NAMES].

The chief spokespersons will together make all decisions around the negotiations process and cost of negotiations, will provide leadership, and make assignments as needed. The chief spokesperson for each party shall be the one authorized to make proposals or counter-proposals. The chief spokespersons shall call for caucus and general sessions, lead the negotiations sessions, and approve tentative agreements.

Negotiations team members will participate as requested by their chief spokesperson in the general sessions and in separate caucus sessions.

For purposes of bargaining, the quorum or minimum number of participants needed to proceed, will be three per side in addition to the chief spokespersons or their designee(s). Caucus sessions may proceed without satisfying this quorum.

6. **Negotiations schedule and hours to be paid.** No bargaining session shall exceed six hours unless mutually agreed by both parties. In general, each day's general negotiations session is planned to start at 9:00 a.m. and end not later than 3:00 p.m. Separate caucus sessions may start earlier or end earlier. Mid-morning and mid-afternoon breaks will be determined by the chief spokespersons based on the flow of the discussion for a given day. In general, these breaks will be planned for close to the mid-point of the morning session and close to the mid-point of the afternoon session. A lunch break will be planned for a minimum of 30 minutes each day.

   A total of eight hours of straight-time pay will be issued to each bargaining unit participant for each day of negotiations, regardless of the duration of that day's session. The only pay exceptions will be for any time away from negotiations for preapproved or protected leave. In such cases, pay will be calculated as a maximum of eight hours minus any hours of preapproved or protected leave. Pay for preapproved or protected leave will be in accordance with the reason for the leave (e.g., PTO, Bereavement Leave, Disability Leave, and so on).

7. **Negotiations assignments.** In general, the chief spokespersons will conduct most bargaining sessions with other negotiations team members in the meeting room to provide background and context as requested by their leadership. The chief spokesperson may elect to ask members of their team to lead their discussion of a topic or set of topics.

   There may be instances in which the chief spokespersons determine they wish to have a sidebar conversation in which their respective team members are not present. In those instances, the team members should remain in their respective caucus rooms so they are ready and available when next needed.

8. **Tentative agreements, final agreements, voting, and ratification.**

- *Tentative agreements (TAs)* are agreements reached in the course of bargaining, which are hoped to be final, but which may change as a means of reaching a final agreement.
- *Final tentative agreement.* Once the parties have bargained each proposal and have reached TAs on each provision that was brought forward, the chief spokespersons will determine that the parties have reached a final tentative agreement on the entire proposed collective bargaining agreement. The chief spokespersons (or their designee) will review the redlined version prior to the union presenting to the membership for a ratification vote.
- *Voting and ratification.* The union will present the proposed new CBA to its members privately in meetings to be held outside of work hours. And the union will conduct a vote of its members to ratify (accept) or reject the proposed new contract. After counting the vote, the union's chief spokesperson will inform the company's chief spokesperson of the result.

9. **Resource personnel/subject matter expert (SME).** There may be occasions that are appropriate for resource personnel and/or SMEs (i.e., individuals who are not part of the bargaining team), to be brought to negotiations periodically and shall be considered a part of the negotiations team.

   SMEs, if used in the bargaining sessions, will be requested by the chief spokesperson(s) to help inform discussions of certain topics. It is expected that any SME would be bargaining unit employees, supervisors, or managers with direct personal experience or knowledge of the topic at hand. SMEs might also be professional employees with special expertise such as the company's human resources professionals who specialize in compensation or benefits. The role of any SME is to provide assistance, data, information, or other topic-specific support identified by the chief spokesperson.

10. **Communication and confidentiality.**

- *Joint external communications.* It is agreed that any information regarding the status of bargaining or mediation shall not be released to the media until bargaining or mediation is complete. Parties must give four working days (Monday through Friday) notice to the other party before releasing anything to the media.

- *Separate communications.* The chief spokesperson(s) will direct the detail of any communication that is not a shared communication and agree that a brief synopsis on how negotiations is going will be acceptable. Negotiations team members are to follow the direction of their leadership with respect to these communications.

- *Confidentiality.* All discussions within the context of negotiations are extremely confidential. All notes and materials used during negotiations are to be kept secure and are not to be shared with anyone not directly involved in the negotiations.

11. **Information requests.** All requests for information are to be made in writing and made with sufficient focus and lead time to allow the data to be collected.

12. **Note taking.** Each party will take its own notes during each session. No audio or video recording is allowed unless specifically pre-approved in writing by the chief spokespersons. Court reporters and stenographers will not be used.

13. **Rules of conduct.** Negotiations participants are to conduct themselves according to the company's existing rules of conduct. If anyone is not respecting the *bargaining rules and guidelines*, the chief spokesperson for that person's team shall request a caucus and discuss the matter with their team member. Sample expectations are shown here:

- *Confidentiality is important.* Bargaining participants are expressly forbidden from discussing bargaining details outside of their respective bargaining teams. Seek direction from your chief spokesperson if questions arise.

- *Attitude and behavior.* Respect each person. All members at the table are to use patience. When interacting with others, focus on the future and not on the past.

- *Communication.* Respect each member of the full bargaining committee. Listen. Really try to understand the other person's point of view by asking clarifying questions. Restate in your own words what you heard for clarification. Be

candid and transparent. Use *I*, not *we, they*, or *you*. No
tip-toeing around. Talk to and not about another person. No
personal attacks.

- *Time and meeting management.* Be present by avoiding
  unnecessary distractions. Silence devices. Step away from the
  meeting if necessary to take a call or respond to a text.

14. **Bargaining sequence**. The chief spokespersons have determined
that bargaining will follow this sequence:

   a. *Bargaining rules and guidelines.* The chief spokespersons will first
   present this bargaining rules and guidelines document to the full
   negotiations teams and answer any clarifying questions.

   b. *Proposals.* The order of discussion will be:

      i. *Status quo articles.* Once these are agreed to, the parties will
      move to noneconomic articles.

      ii. *Noneconomic articles.* These will be discussed after both par-
      ties have had the opportunity to reach tentative agreement on
      their status quo articles. Once the noneconomic articles are
      agreed to, the parties will move to economic articles.

      iii. *Economic articles.* These will be discussed after both parties
      have had the opportunity to present their noneconomic
      articles.

   c. *Who presents first?* In each group of the previous proposals, the
   union will present its proposals first. After the union has presented all of its proposals in a given group, the company will
   present its list of proposed changes and will respond to clarifying
   questions from the union's side.

   d. *Tentative agreements, modify, or withdraw.* For each initial proposal presented, the other party is to respond with their position
   with or without discussion of the initial proposal. They are to
   clearly state whether they are tentatively accepting the proposal
   or offering a modified or counter-proposal. The first party will
   respond similarly or may choose to withdraw their proposal.

   While tentative acceptances of proposals are permitted, they
   are not binding until the total agreement is approved by both
   parties' constituents. All tentative agreements must be signed off
   by the chief spokespersons on all proposed changes until a final
   tentative agreement of the full CBA has been achieved.

15. **Terms and conditions**. The terms and conditions of the present collective bargaining agreement shall remain in full force and effect until a successor collective bargaining agreement is ratified by the union membership and signed by all parties.

Agreed to this _____ day of MM/YYYY by the chief spokespersons:

_____   _____

COMPANY CHIEF SPOKESPERSON   UNION CHIEF SPOKESPERSON
NAME   NAME
NAME OF COMPANY   NAME OF UNION, LOCAL #_____
JOB TITLE   JOB TITLE

APPENDIX D

Management's Chief Spokesperson's Opening Remarks—Sample

First opening remarks. These should be made early on, before any proposal is handed across the table. The objective here is to be welcoming and aspirational, set the tone for bargaining, set big picture expectations, and acknowledge that concerns may exist. The primary audience members that you are speaking to are the employee members of the union's bargaining committee.

Sample Opening Remarks for First Session

I think you all know me, but just to be sure, let me introduce myself. I'm [NAME AND TITLE] for the company. I'll be management's chief spokesperson. [NAME] and [NAME] will also be speaking from time to time as will probably each member of management's negotiations team.

I want to thank everyone on both teams for all the work they have already done to prepare for negotiations as well as all the work that is ahead of us. Several people here have participated in our negotiations in the past. Others have not participated in any labor agreement negotiations. Your experience comes mostly from your current active roles in our labor–management relationship. I mention this simply to illustrate that different ones of us are starting at different places for this round of negotiations, and I ask that we all be patient with each other as we get this round of bargaining underway.

The parties have agreed to use a traditional process of bargaining. I expect that the chief spokesperson for each side will do much of the talking. That said, we still need to give ourselves permission to ask process questions and to break into our caucus sessions. When we are in this room together, we're in a formal session and each of us must follow the agreed-upon process.

You will see that management is not asking for many changes. One of our goals is to work with the union to find ways to stabilize things for the bargaining unit employees so there is less churn and more predictability about things that can be predictable. I appreciate that the union will be telling us concerns on a few topics. I'm guessing that we won't always agree to what is being requested because we have an obligation to balance any request with a number of other considerations for which management is also accountable. Remember that our company is a publicly traded company, so we have to consider our shareholders as well as our customers and employees. Sometimes it's a lot to balance.

I can assure you that the company is committed to the best possible outcome for our employees (your members). We are committed to providing family-wage jobs, competitive benefits, the right staffing levels, and opportunities for employees to grow and be involved.

With that, let's get started.

Opening remarks for second session. This assumes noneconomics have been settled and that the parties are ready to begin bargaining economic items. These comments should be made before any economic proposal is handed across the table. The objective here is to be aspirational, to set expectations about "the pie," to describe the pie, and to explain the concept of "bundling." It is important to be frank and transparent. The primary audience members that you are speaking to are the employee members of the union's bargaining committee.

Sample Remarks to Start Second Session

I'd like to welcome everyone back to the table and congratulate all of us on completing the noneconomics. Thank you, everyone, for all the work you've done to get us this far. I'm optimistic that we'll be able to close out the economic pieces in the remaining days that we have calendared.

I want to talk a little about "the pie" because the concept might be new to some people. The pie refers to the full cost of every change through the life of the contract. The pie is the pie. It won't get any bigger, but we can talk about changing the portions of the pie. For example, if we agree to add a holiday, that's a cost to the company. Every employee would get that holiday and, to provide coverage to our customers, other employees will have to fill in on that shift, most likely at a higher rate of pay than regular straight-time pay. So, we do the math of what that would look like for the life of the contract, and that gives us a projected cost for adding one holiday. In a little while, you'll see our counter-proposal on holidays where we suggest staying with the status quo and not adding an additional holiday.

We could put more money into one area; however, it needs to come out of a different area, otherwise we would be expanding the pie and we may not expand the pie. Why is that? We need to balance expectations from our shareholders, customers, employees, and other stakeholders. We are committed to providing family-wage jobs, competitive benefits, the right staffing levels, and opportunities for employees to grow and be involved.

I think we did a great job finding common ground in our discussions of noneconomics. And I'm confident that by staying focused on our top priorities, we can find common ground on economics.

I'd like to speak to our economic counter-proposal before we hand it to you. We have nine economic articles to discuss and today we are going to give you our counter on just four of them. Let me say first that we see four of these articles as items we can probably get agreement on pretty quickly and independently of the others.

Then there are five articles that we are presenting as a "bundle." By that I mean that they are closely connected, they are integrated, and we ask that they be discussed together. Changes to one of these five will likely mean a change to one or more of the others of the five. No carve-outs. We are looking for the union to either agree or counter as a bundle.

Any questions? If not, let's get started.

APPENDIX E

Saying "No" in Economics

When responding to a union's economic proposal, *never* use the wording *we cannot afford to …* or anything like that. Doing so would allow the union to assert that you are pleading poverty. They would ask to see your organization's detailed financials. The NLRB typically supports a union's request for financials. It would be very problematic to step back once you say that the organization cannot afford something.

Instead, be sure that management's team members have been briefed on what to say and not to say regarding economics. Here are some appropriate responses[3] for management to use when rejecting any of the union's economic proposals:

- The market doesn't bear it.
- We already have very competitive _____.
- That is not a good use of our resources.
- That is not the most efficient use of our resources.
- We would rather accomplish this either with the status quo and/or another way (provide a proposal).

---

[3] *These examples are courtesy of Burdzinski & Partners. More information at www.burdzinski.com.*

APPENDIX F

Resources

Books

Helpful although often brief discussion of the planning and preparing aspects of labor agreement negotiations is in these recommended books:

Better, M.B. 1993. *Contract Bargaining Handbook for Local Union Leaders.* Arlington, VA: Bloomberg BNA.

Cassel, R.M. 2010. *Negotiating a Labor Contract: A Management Handbook, Fourth Edition.* Arlington, VA: Bloomberg BNA.

Fisher, R. and D. Shapiro. 2006. *Beyond Reason: Using Emotions as You Negotiate.* New York, NY: Penguin Books.

Fisher, R. and W. Ury (authors), with B. Patton, ed. 2011. *Getting to Yes: Negotiating Agreement Without Giving In.* New York: Penguin Books. Originally published 1981.

Ury, W. 2007. *The Power of a Positive No: Save the Deal, Save the Relationship— and Still Say No.* New York, NY: Bantam Books.

Wheeler, M. 2013. *The Art of Negotiation: How to Improvise Agreement in a Chaotic World.* New York, NY: Simon & Schuster.

Consultants and Attorneys

- Burdzinski & Partners, Inc.
  www.burdzinski.com.
  A federal labor practice: labor relations specialists, nonlawyers, agents, and advocates for employers.
- Littler Mendelson P.C.
  www.littler.com.
  Largest law firm in the world focusing exclusively on representing management in employment, employee benefits, and labor law matters.

- Restructuring Associates, Inc.
  www.restructassoc.com.
  Support for labor–management relationships including training for interest-based bargaining.

Websites

- www.dol.gov/agencies/olms.
  The Office of Labor-Management Statistics publishes information that is useful for management's strike planning in particular. The OLMS is responsible for enforcing the Labor Management Reporting and Disclosure Act, which requires labor unions to file annual reports detailing their operations. You can get the union local's LM-2, LM-3, or LM-4 forms at this site.
- www.fmcs.gov
  The Federal Mediation and Conciliation Service's mission is to preserve and promote labor–management peace and cooperation. This is the entity that receives the F-7 notice of intent to bargain putting them on notice that if the parties' CBA bargaining becomes strained, they may be asked to help mediate. In addition to being on standby for possible mediation services, they offer joint training on how to bargain a CBA.
- www.nlrb.gov
  The National Labor Relations Board enforces the bargaining requirements of the Taft–Hartley Act. Management's Three Musketeers team must have a solid understanding of the rules of bargaining called out in Section 8.
- www.unionfacts.com
  Source for facts and statistics about the union and specific local you will be bargaining with. Strike fund (often called "strike benefit") information is here.

References

Better, M.B. Revised by K. May. 2017. *Contract Bargaining Handbook for Local Union Leaders.* Arlington, VA: Bloomberg BNA.

Cassel, R.M. 2010. *Negotiating a Labor Contract: A Management Handbook,* Fourth Ed. Arlington, VA: Bloomberg BNA.

Fisher, R. and D. Shapiro. 2006. *Beyond Reason: Using Emotions as You Negotiate.* New York, NY: Penguin Books.

Fisher, R. and W. Ury (authors), with B. Patton, ed. 2011. *Getting to Yes: Negotiating Agreement Without Giving In.* New York, NY: Penguin Books. Originally published 1981.

Hindle, T. 1998. *Negotiating Skills.* New York, NY: DK Publishing.

Luecke, R. 2003. *Negotiation.* Boston: Harvard Business School Publishing Corporation.

Malhotra, D. and M.H. Bazerman. 2008. *Negotiation Genius.* New York, NY: Bantam Dell.

Ury, W. 2007. *The Power of a Positive No: Save the Deal, Save the Relationship—and Still Say No.* New York, NY: Bantam Books.

Wheeler, M. 2013. *The Art of Negotiation: How to Improvise Agreement in a Chaotic World.* New York, NY: Simon & Schuster.

Online References

UnionFacts. n.d. **www.unionfacts.com.**

U.S. Bureau of Labor Statistics. n.d. **www.bls.gov.**

U.S. Federal Mediation and Conciliation Service. n.d. **www.fmcs.gov.**

U.S. National Labor Relations Bureau. n.d. **www.nlrb.gov.**

U.S. Office of Labor-Management Statistics. n.d. **www.dol.gov/agencies/olms.**

About the Author

Kathy Beyerchen has 20+ years of private sector labor experience with publicly traded and privately held corporations ranging in size from a Fortune 250 company to a small agricultural cooperative. In these human resources roles, she facilitated management's negotiating teams for collective bargaining agreements with some of the largest unions in the country as well as some lesser-known unions. Kathy holds a Masters in Labor and Human Resources from Ohio State University and a BA in History and Political Science from the University of California, Santa Barbara. She held her Senior Professional in Human Resources certification for 20 years. Kathy owned and operated an award-winning independent staffing agency, and co-owned and operated a highly successful commercial beekeeping business, both of which greatly shaped her negotiating talents and processes. She can be reached at KathyBeyerchen@Kathy Beyerchen.com.

Index

Made in the USA
Middletown, DE
27 August 2024

59861101R00075